Paid For

Common Sense Financial Guides for the Average American

Bob Jennings CPA

ISBN:1543198902
ISBN-13:9781543198904

FORWARD

10,000 tax returns. 40 years of dealing with average Americans. 35 years of listening to the financial "experts" with their supposed secrets, get rich quick schemes and advice that works really well in books but is rarely followed in real life. I've had enough. There are no secrets here. There are no get rich quick or retire early scams or schemes, and in particular there are none of those academic ideas that don't apply in real life. This book is about a lifetime of dealing with average people who just want to know what to do for now, their future and their kids. Much like the old-time family doctor of a bygone age, this book is written by an old-time family CPA with knowledge of the latest tools and tricks, but the experience of 40 years of listening to problems and preparing 10,000 tax returns to give you some real, hands-on advice, maybe with some stories, humor, and life lessons to help you avoid the financial mistakes of life.

This book is dedicated to the 10,000 clients. No real names are used.

CONTENTS

ACKNOWLEDGMENTS

Former clients, family and friends, some of whom who are no longer with us, provided the experience I needed to write this book. Thank you. Mike Gorrell, I sure miss you and your ability to laugh at adversity. Anne Rice, Ruth McKinley and Cindy Pierce-three intelligent, strong willed women who trusted my advice and taught me about being responsible with that advice. Bill Julius, Walt Bales and Ira McKinley the three men who showed me how to run a business ethically and profitably. Bob & Mary Rose Jennings who taught me right from wrong by example, even though it took a while to settle in. Louis L'Amour for building a young man's character through fiction. And most importantly to Jean Jennings for that common-sense stability that a lifetime of love brings to a man with no direction. Thank you and the thousands of other fine people who guided me down this road, lived with my mistakes and big mouth, and most of all paid me to give me the experience!

1
PAID FOR

About ten years ago, one of my friends asked me why I drove an old Dodge truck with 180,000 miles on it when I, a car nut, could afford something nicer. My response, and the first time I can ever remember saying it, was that there were two key financial words in life: *"paid for"*, and that's where the idea for this book began. He asked me if I ever had a car loan. The answer in short was yes, and at one point the car loans were more than our house payments. This chapter is about recognizing what *"paid for"* really means. We also introduce you to three terms: *steel debt trap* (car loans); *income tax blindness* (letting taxes drive your decision making); and *TFM* or *Terminal Financial Mistakes* (which is multiple bad financial moves based on lack of knowledge or poor decision making).

The Steel Debt Trap and Sacrifice

From an accountant's point of view buying a personal car is the absolute worst big-dollar investment most Americans will ever make. A steel debt trap. Think about it-a new car costs more than most Americans will make in 6-8 months of working, goes down in value the day we buy it, continues to decline in value while we own it, and requires substantial amounts of money to maintain and operate this thing. We then must pay hundreds of dollars to the state for tags and plates for the privilege of owning the car and thousands of dollars every year for insurance in case we wreck this steel debt trap that keeps going down in value! And yet, we continue to buy new cars, mortgaging our future to these always-depreciating bolt collections on wheels and we borrow the money for five, six and even seven years in a never-ending downward spiral of wasted money.

We buy a car for many reasons, primarily the ability to get back and forth to work, and secondarily for the events of life, such as kids, shopping and leisure. We also buy cars as a psychological reward in a country that recognizes cars as social statements in addition to transportation. Do we really want to buy cars that cost so much and return so little that they hinder our retirement, or college, or any other more useful purpose?

I went to college at Colorado State with a fellow that, like me, loved cars, especially muscle and sports cars. We did not know each other then, but coincidentally met ten years later when he was living in Southern Indiana and called me to do his tax return. Jerry (not his real name) had been involved in a horrible car accident right after college and was severely physically disabled, but he had a mind that was as sharp as any scientist. For several years, with great difficulty, he could work in a good job, but eventually Jerry was forced to retire as fully disabled.

Jerry and I got along extremely well, I think because I didn't patronize or minimalize his disabilities, and because we good-naturedly bantered back and forth as only good friends can do about cars, politics, and yes, disabilities. Jerry gave me a lot of grief about the front steps of my building and was the first person I knew to make me recognize the effects disabilities can have on mobility. We added a wheelchair ramp to that old office building because Jerry's physical issues opened my eyes to the need.

Jerry lived vicariously through sports cars owned by others, and, combined with his love for music and electronic sound systems, knew more about sports cars and electronics than anyone I ever met. He always drove a conservative old Chevy that was easy for him to enter and exit. We argued for hours comparing my Mopar muscle cars against his Corvettes. Jerry was fiercely independent and refused help as much as he could. One day he came to my office building and laboriously entered the building and negotiated the steps, the parking and the elevator. When he entered my office, he was bursting with excitement and could barely contain himself. His physical disabilities also made him hard to understand when he spoke, but I understood that he had a new car he wanted me to see.

We then re-negotiated the steps, the elevator and the doors and went back out to the parking lot where I was shocked by the sight of a brand new red Corvette. Jerry was visibly excited to show me the car, explain all the buttons and gadgets and talk about its power and maneuverability. When he got into the driver's seat to give me a ride, he entered with extreme difficulty and I immediately asked him about the payments and his future with a car he might not be able to use. I learned a lot that day from Jerry when he told me he would sacrifice anything he could to own this car. You see, no accountant would mortgage his future for a car he might not be able to use in six months. But for Jerry this Corvette wasn't a steel debt trap, it was a release. Jerry beat the steel debt trap by choosing psychology over practicality. Jerry taught me that *"Paid For"* means <u>sacrificing</u> something. For most of us *"Paid For"* is about financial cost, for some people it is about psychological cost, but for all of us it is about sacrifice of some type.

Jerry drove that Vette for about eighteen months before his disabilities forced him to give it up. Like some of my other less-mobile client friends, I went to Jerry's house for his tax season appointment to get his information, eat lunch, visit, pet his dog and give him grief about the Corvette in the garage, but we loved every minute of it and I looked forward to the visit and the regular phone calls and letters during the year. On the last appointment I had with Jerry I went to his home to get his stuff and meet, and I rang the doorbell several times to no answer. His little dog was barking frantically at me but I was too stupid to recognize the signs, and mistakenly assumed Jerry had a different appointment away from home at a doctor's or something. As a normally aggressive, first-to-act person I still regret not breaking down the door. Unknown to me, Jerry had fallen in the shower and eventually passed away before he was found several days later. To this day, I am haunted by the chance that maybe I could have saved him, but I will never know. Jerry's memory is what shines through however, and the brightness in Jerry's eyes when he showed me that car is what I can still see today. Thank you, Jerry, for that lesson.

But back to the steel debt trap. If you are buying a car for a psychological satisfaction, then ignore what follows. For the rest of us, consider what you are looking for in a car, and in what order: safety (as a grandparent we now put that first!); comfort; cost; and style. If you can put style in the list, but not first, let's look at a few simple financial aspects of car ownership, remembering always *"Paid For"*.

When I was about thirty I realized that I was buying a different car every couple of years, borrowing the trade-in difference, and slowly digging a steel debt trap that was a life-long spiral of car loans with increasing balances unless something changed. It shocked me to see where I had gone from paying cash for my first (used) car to using up that equity with each trade, so that by age thirty I owed as much on the cars as they were worth. The only way out of the steel debt trap was to keep the cars until they were both paid for and older.

My thirtieth birthday was the day I decided to change, and every extra dollar for the next two years went to paying off those car loans. At the same time, I swore we would never buy another car with borrowed money. My wife and I sacrificed vacations and home improvements to dig out of that hole. The funny thing is that the cars ran just fine for several more years each, and because I maintained them well they continued to be safe transportation that was just a little out of style.

Cars are consumables like groceries, and the sooner we recognize that they are consumables the better off our situation becomes. To this day, we still love cars, but my wife drives a ten-year-old hybrid Ford which we will only trade when she is ready, on something that is safe, yet stylish and cost effective. I drive a four-year-old pickup with no plans to do anything for the future, and yes, we paid the cash difference for both.

To those folks who say *"I can borrow the money at 0% from the manufacturer and that it is a better deal financially"*, I agree with the financial aspect, but after forty years of practice I have learned many things, one of which is that *if you miss a zero percent interest payment they can still repossess the car*. The psychological side of a debt-free car offsets whatever inconsequential interest you may earn by investing the cash you held on to, and in my experience, it is the rare person who actually invests that cash difference. If you can't pay for it without borrowing, don't buy it. Avoid the steel debt trap!

You will also hear people say "*never buy a new car because of the instant depreciation the minute you drive off the lot*". There is a lot of truth to that statement, but it ignores another psychological aspect of car ownership: reliability and warranty. When my wife and I buy cars today, we do consider new cars in our household, understanding that the cost is higher, but that the reliability and safety factors should also be considered, and now that we haul grandkids around frankly we are usually willing to pay for a new car for the additional peace of mind

For those of you who take money out on a home equity line to buy a car "because of the tax savings" hear this loud and clear from a CPA-ARE YOU OUT OF YOUR MIND? You are jeopardizing your house to buy an investment that is so bad that it continually declines in value, costs thousands of dollars to keep and operate and has minimal equity to theoretically save a few tax dollars. Folks, I am in the business of being an income tax professional and there are absolutely, absolutely no circumstances that a few theoretical dollars of tax savings offset the risks involved in mortgaging your house for an asset that is guaranteed to decline in value. I have no problem with taking a risk in an investment, but I have a major problem with taking risks for negative returns. A basic concept of investing is risk/return, and borrowing against your home to buy a daily-driver car incurs great risk with absolutely no possible return. Here is a blunter analogy:

For the average American their home will be one of their two major lifetime assets, along with a retirement account. A home almost always increases in value if kept in good repair, and provides a financial cushion and retreat point far into old age. If you want to borrow against it to increase its value through improvements I have no problem with that. Would you want to borrow against it however to hire a backhoe to dig a hole in the yard? No, of course not, because that would incur great risk to the home *and* reduce the value of the home. When you are borrowing against your home to buy a car you are digging that hole folks.

I also say the tax savings are theoretical because people subject to the alternative minimum tax get no deduction for the interest-they are risking their home to make an investment that will always lose value, for a tax deduction that has disappeared! Brilliant. I will tell you this, no experienced tax professional that really understands home equity interest deductions and risk/return will ever recommend using equity lines for cars. *Sacrifice* and drive your existing car another year, or buy an older or cheaper car. If your tax expert recommends this move for the tax deduction my advice is change tax preparers.

Americans are stricken with a financially fatal disease I call *income tax blindness*. We are constantly told something we buy is "tax-deductible". Here is some common-sense advice on *income tax blindness*: income tax effects should be the last part of a decision to spend money, not the first part. WE DON'T HAVE A 100% INCOME TAX RATE IN THIS COUNTRY! What does this mean? It means the individual in the highest tax bracket in America that spends $1,000 on a "tax-deductible" item is still out of pocket $1,000 dollars. You see, the highest tax rate we have is around 35%, so if you spend $1,000 on a "tax deduction" it will save you $350 in tax dollars, but you will still be out of pocket $1,000. You will have saved $350 in tax (but still spent the money) and spent another $650 to buy the item. The primary decision should be "Do I need this item?", not "is it tax deductible"

This analogy is as appropriate in business as it is in individual decisions. If you are buying a car *with borrowed money* because there is a tax deduction for the car or the sales tax, or there is a tax credit for buying an electric car, you have two deadly financial diseases: *income tax blindness* and *steel debt trap* disease, and you are in the advanced stages of a disease I call *terminal financial mistakes* or *TFM*.

What about leasing a car? SouthBay Ford's Los Angeles website shows a new 2017 Ford Fusion lease for 36 months at $239 monthly for 36 months with a $2,000 down payment and a top credit rating, or a purchase price of $22,995, or $21,495 if financed with available 72 month, 0% interest rate financing (about $300 monthly). Leasing of course means low payments, no equity and minimal maintenance. It is ideal for those individuals who put style ahead of everything else-they get a new car every three years at a lesser cost than buying and trading every three years! It is a poor decision overall in that the cost is still much higher than buying and owning a car for many years.

How do the numbers work out? Let's do a simple analysis over 9 years. We will assume no gas costs since it will be the same for all cars; 3 lease vehicles during the lease term; 2 trades for the steel debt trap buyer and the same car for all nine years for the person following my advice. The steel debt trap buyer will have negative equity after three years and will need a $2,000 down payment with each trade. Repairs and maintenance for the first 3 years of ownership we will assume is the same for all three approaches; but does apply to the 9-year ownership car in years 4-9, and is more than offset by reduced insurance and licensing costs. Finally, we will assume similar lease terms for all three lease cars, and a 10% down payment for the steel debt trap buyer. We ignore the time value of money for several reasons including minimal inflation now, psychological value of a *"paid for"* car, and the real-life fact that few people actually invest any savings on the car purchase! For the real critic, go ahead and build it in, 9 years of ownership is still easily the best choice.

	Lease	Trade every 3 years	Same car all years
Yr 1 down payment	$2,000	$0	$22,995
Year 1 payments	2,880	3,600	0
Year 2 Payments	2,880	3,600	0
Year 3 Payments	2,880	3,600	0
3 years licensing & Insurance	4,500	4,500	4,500
Yr 4 down payment	2,000	2,000	0
Year 4 payments	2,880	3,600	0
Year 5 payments	2,880	3,600	0
Year 6 payments	2,880	3,600	0
3 years licensing & insurance	4,500	4,500	3,000
Same car 3 years maintenance	0	0	1,000
Yr 7 down payment	2,000	2,000	0
Year 7 payments	2,880	3,600	0
Year 8 payments	2,880	3,600	0
Year 9 payments	2,880	3,600	0
3 years licensing & insurance	4,500	4,500	2,000
Same car 3 years maintenance	0	0	1,500
Equity after 9 years	0	0	-5,000
Net cost after 9 years	$45,420	$49,900	$29,995

Credit Cards and Installment Debts (such as furniture)

The easy availability of credit combined with the disconnect between cash and debt has led many Americans astray on credit cards through a loss of control of their own finances. Credit card debt can be avoided by first avoiding their ease of use (not having them), and secondarily reverting to a cash based model of consumption. Debit cards are not a cash based model-they are an enabler to incur credit card debt through your loss of impulse purchase control. **Revert to a cash model and carry just enough cash to meet your needs, and pay your other bills online to retain control of your own finances-AVOID DEBIT CARD USE-they are too easy to use and lose control of your budget-WRITE A CHECK!**

Are you a religious person? Then credit cards are issued by Satan! If you are not a religious person, then credit cards are issued by Scrooge and the bad banker in “It’s a Wonderful Life”. These multi-tentacled octopus’ of debt are one of the absolute worst things a consumer can have and should be limited to one card for emergencies. DO NOT CARRY A CREDIT CARD WITH YOU unless you can pay it off every month.

Impulse purchases are made possible with credit and debit cards, and if you only carry cash then you will be able to resist the impulse. The temptation, in my experience, when added to an American desire for instant gratification leads to TFM. Own one credit card, leave it home, use it for emergencies and pay it off every month. The same applies to debit cards-they are too easy to use and are a device invented by retailers to promote sales through the instant gratification approach. One easy tool is available to the average consumer: the cash only model stops impulse purchases; and cash is easy to monitor to control debt-you can't spend more than you've got! **Using cash for daily expenses returns the control of your finances to you-use checks for every bill!**

If you are already saddled with loads of credit card debt, here is what to do. First, get a second job. You read that right, it's time to grow a backbone and face the bad decisions and impulse purchases you made in the past to avoid them in the future. Second, cut up every single card but the one with the lowest interest rate and highest limit. Third, never, ever, ever apply for any credit cards again-use just this one. Fourth, don't carry the card with you until you have it paid off and can pay it off every month-it is for emergencies only, and going out to dinner isn't an emergency. And fifth, start paying off the cards. Set up a spreadsheet showing the current balance, and then set up a budget of the extra income applied to the loans as discussed below.

But Bob, won't having only one credit card and paying it off every month hurt my credit score? Let's see-what do you need a credit score for? Oh yeah, to borrow more money, exactly what we are trying to avoid. Having just one high-limit card and using it responsibly will have minimal effect on your credit score.

Many advisors will tell you to pay off the highest rate cards first, and I tentatively agree with that. However, there is an incredible psychological feeling of accomplishment to paying off any card, so I would consider paying off a couple of low balance cards first, just for the satisfaction. This concept is like the instant weight loss promised by Marie Osmond in TV ads: Nutri-System understands the psychological benefit of instant results, and you should too. So, if you have several cards, pay off a couple of low balance ones to get that instant gratification, and then hit the high interest one third. Use every dime of the second job's income to pay towards the debt to remind you what you were doing.

There are no miracles to credit card debt relief. Pay them off through hard work and financial sacrifice. Debt renegotiation programs are horrible ideas at a great cost in terms of credit ratings, cost of the programs (which are often scams) and frankly the lack of responsibility the programs teach. I have never met a successful person that did not acknowledge their own debts-they maybe were financially successful, but they were not people I would want to associate with or have my grandkids date. Success is not measured financially it is measured by the relationships we develop. Would you rather your obituary read "he made a lot of money" or "she was loved and respected by everyone she met?"

When you get the cards paid off (your goal should be 24 months or less), then how about continuing with that second job for another year or two, banking the money you were spending every month for credit card debt payments to build a nest egg for the future? You won't get any sympathy here for working a second job-it won't hurt you. And don't ever use another credit card unless you are absolutely certain you can pay it off at the end of the month.

Home Mortgages

OK, we are at the only area where you must borrow money. Here are some basic rules to start. First, if your home mortgage requires that you pay for principal mortgage insurance (PMI) you have no business buying a home. PMI insurance is insurance that *the homeowner pays for* that protects the lender in case you default-they recognize you are a poor risk with not enough equity and they want protection against your deadbeat-ness. Hello, McFly-is there a lesson here? Of course, there is-you should not have bought the home. As a general rule to avoid paying for PMI you need a twenty percent down payment on the home.

Second, obtain your home mortgage from a local bank that does not resell the mortgages to a third party. (Ask the bank). It may cost you a touch more in interest but you will be dealing with a local bank that is much, much, much more likely to deal with any problems than some faceless multi-national bank. I know this goes against the common thinking of getting the best interest rate by searching online. I am giving you practical advice from forty years of dealing with home mortgage problems for clients, STAY LOCAL and pay a bit more. Come on folks, listen to this advice, it comes from experience and is free advice from a CPA-words not usually used in the same sentence "free" and "CPA". If you go to the local bank's home loan officer first you do not need a mortgage broker, who I guarantee will get you a lower rate, but with a national lender that will repackage your loan five times over the next five years to some out of state entity. STAY LOCAL.

Third, your lifelong goal should be to have your mortgage ***PAID FOR*** by age 65. Period. This means no thirty-year mortgages after you turn 35 years old. I can hear the screams now, "But I can't afford the house without a thirty-year mortgage". Hey guess what, you are right, you can't afford the house. And buying or refinancing a house at age 50 or later with a thirty-year mortgage-why don't you send me your own nomination for my financial dumber than snot award. Are there exceptions to this rule? I suppose, but you need to convince me that the retirement income left to your spouse after you die will be enough to pay that mortgage when your widow is eighty and needing nursing care with limited income.

Over forty years of practice I noticed a great tendency summarized by looking at three lines on a tax return. The people with a huge deduction on Schedule A for mortgage interest never seemed to have any numbers on the two lines reserved for interest or dividend income. These same folks at age sixty suddenly realized that they were going to be forced to rely on Social Security and a little bit of retirement while stuck with a huge (but gorgeous) home, an incredible mortgage payment, and little in the way of assets. My rule is inflexible-***PAID FOR*** by age sixty-five, and yes, I follow that rule myself.

Fourth, in owning a home, pride of ownership must be present to increase the value of the home. This means neat, clean yards and well-maintained homes. It doesn't mean every toy and tool is put away at all times, but it does mean that you are keeping up with problems rather than catching up with problems. Any realtor or real estate investor will tell you about pride of ownership and the value it adds to a home. Keep the grass cut, the shrubs trimmed and the stuff put away as much as possible so that you don't have to catch up. Have you ever noticed on those home sale TV shows that there is no clutter and everything is cut, trimmed and cleaned? There is a reason-pride of ownership.

Fifth, don't use your home equity as a bank, except for things that will increase the value of the home or your family, while not increasing risk. What I am talking about here is home equity lines. A home equity line for home improvements and emergencies is fine. A home equity line used for kid's colleges is acceptable if it is ***PAID FOR*** by age 65. A home equity line for debt consolidation, buying cars or consumption is a ridiculous move in nearly every case, as discussed in our steel debt trap discussion. All the experts will tell you to consolidate with a home equity line. I disagree 100% with that advice because I have the practical experience of 10,000 tax returns, which is better than any textbook. You are risking the one asset you have to pay off debts that will not take your house if disaster strikes. Don't do it, even if it saves one hundred dollars every month, in forty years of practice I have seen too many homes repossessed from using equity lines. Here is a real-life story from my CPA firm years ago.

Calvert and Becky (not real names) both worked and enjoyed excellent incomes working in the office of a national company. They had a beautiful home, drove modern BMW equivalent cars and traveled extensively. Good for them. Behind the scenes however I saw that these fifty-somethings had a very large mortgage on the house, owed as much as the cars were worth, and had absolutely no interest or dividend income. One day they were approached by a mortgage broker touting the tax benefits of "using their home equity" to pay off the cars and credit cards while deducting the interest. *You need to recognize that a mortgage broker makes money by selling (closing) a loan-they do NOT have your best interests at heart.* When Becky called me, and asked my advice I strongly emphasized I thought it was a horrible idea, and that the tax savings were a sales tool, not a real benefit.

Calvert and Becky were so offended by my advice that they left me as clients. Sadly, a few months later their employer closed their local office and Becky lost her job, soon followed by Calvert. They had some retirement money that they lived on, but it was not enough to make the house payment <u>and</u> the equity line payment and eleven months later their home was foreclosed upon. If they had left the cars financed through the car loan companies, the cars would have been repossessed, but they could have kept the house since they did have enough retirement savings to make the standard mortgage payment. Lesson learned? Do not jeopardize your home for a tax deduction. Do not take tax advice from someone who only makes money when they sell you the item they give advice about. Do not let mortgage brokers make your financial decisions: make your own and see if the local bank can help.

Sixth, when buying a home do not buy a home that is financed by the seller. The risk is too great. Oftentimes younger Americans cannot make a down payment on a home they want and they allow the builder or homeowner to finance the home for them in a “real estate contract”. Now don’t get me wrong, I have seen many real estate contracts work out fine, my wife and I even bought our own first home using one. But I have also seen many go badly wrong, usually for the buyer.

Over the years, I have seen buyers in real estate contracts make payments to the seller, who in turn had their own mortgage on the home. The original mortgage prohibited the existing owner from selling or assigning the loan and the new buyer threw their payments away when the lender discovered the illegal assignment. I have seen contract buyers make payments for 8-10 months to the seller, who in turn did not make payments to the bank and then the home was repossessed. I have seen buyers that did not understand the loan amortization agreement and ended up owing more than they planned for, and I have seen buyers that had homes foreclosed when the seller (or legal owner) did not pay the property tax. I have seen buyers that have had their contract home burn down, only to find that they had totally inadequate insurance to cover the contents. In summary, the bad stories have taught me that if you cannot get a conventional loan, don’t buy the home in most cases.

Finally, what about paying off your home early by paying extra principal every two weeks? This is a nice conservative financial move that I tend to agree with on one hand, but with which I disagree on the other hand depending on the situation. If you are in an area of the country which normally experiences rapid home appreciation, I think it is a good idea to keep reducing the principal with extra payments. For example, if you have a 2% mortgage interest rate and the home increases in value by 10% every year you are achieving an amazing, tax-free return on the principal payments so keep doing it. If you are in the rest of the country that experiences slight home value increases every year I think I would put my extra money somewhere else that would offer a greater return.

So now you have my clearly biased guidance on what to do with home mortgages. For many of you the advice is excellent going in, but you haven’t bought your first home yet. Maybe you are just married, or just entering the workforce or re-entering the workforce, and you are faced with the problem most people will face: how do I come up with the down payment? Let me tell you a little story again.

In late 1978 I had just graduated from my Master’s program and my wife and I wanted to buy a home. Our parents were unable to help us in any way and, although we both had good jobs, we were not making enough money to really save for a down payment.

There are only three options for anyone at this point: continue to rent forever; or reduce expenses; or come up with more money. This is not touchy-feely politically correct crap here, there is only one choice. I got a second job working evenings for a local CPA firm and a third job working Saturdays teaching at a local university. My wife got a second job working evenings and weekends in a retail job. Within 15 months we had saved $10,000, enough for a 20% down payment on a $50,000 home, bought on contract in April, 1980 from a friend of my family. For those folks who laugh and say today this would not be enough, those amounts in today's dollars would be an equivalent of a little over $75,000 down payment on a $400,000 home, so don't tell me it cannot be done. ***PAID FOR*** means sacrifice, and a little sacrifice was necessary to achieve what we wanted.

The funniest thing about those early sacrifices were the lifelong effects that they had. We have all heard the old homily about the harder you work, the luckier you are. Many times I have heard my family members say how lucky I am financially. Well what they don't realize is that forty years later I am still working a three-job equivalent, so yes, I guess I am lucky. The habits developed early are the habits that will determine financial stability in the future. I was taught by a hard but brilliant man, my Dad, and he made me pay him rent when I got my first job as a teenager, until I got married many years later. I paid for my own college and graduate school by sacrificing and working in a car dealership and a family business during the day and weekends while attending college at night. That early life lesson in sacrifice led to this book and instilled the discipline necessary to learn, earn and now pass this knowledge to you in ***PAID FOR.***

2
SAVING AT THE BEGINNING

Why do you need to save at all? All experts tell us that everyone needs a safety fund. I agree wholeheartedly with that statement. This is not the fund you use to buy a house, or a car or pay for college, it is that fund you know is there for any emergency. I don't necessarily agree with the expert guidance of three months' worth of expenses put aside in savings, because that is too hard to quantify, so I recommend $10,000. In this chapter, we will show you how to get there.

The hardest part of saving money is starting to save money.

Some general guidance is a good beginning. Saving must be made as easy as possible, while withdrawal must be fairly difficult. Why should withdrawals be difficult? Because at the beginning if the savings account is easy to access, then it is too easy to spend, and that's what we want to avoid. Secondly, saving money must start small before it becomes large. We will give you a plan, but first let's jump into saving money.

Let's start at the simplest level. My wife and I began this next practice over forty years ago, and we still do it today. Begin with a cash based model of activity. Get a large glass pickle jar, or a large white plastic container-you want to be able to see inside it so you can watch it grow. This physical symbolism of saving is where we start our plan. At the end of every single day, empty your change into that jar. It will become such a habit that it will soon become automatic when you come home from work, and you won't feel its absence. Don't laugh because it does work, we still do it today, and every year we get several hundred dollars out of that jar at Christmas. For the naysayers that laugh at this simple idea-what do you have to show for your change?

A prime lesson exists in this simple plan as a key to saving money, the statement "you won't feel it's absence." Saving money can be painless if you allow it to be painless. You start with a simple system that you don't even notice, and then go from there to more involved savings programs. Save first, not last with leftovers.

OK, our next step in saving money is a detailed budget. Without a budget identifying when money comes in, when it goes out, and projected shortfalls and excesses it is nearly impossible to begin saving money. If I had one key piece of financial advice for a young person (or persons) starting out in the world it would be to develop a budget and then try to stick with it, and for older folks it is never too late to start.

Several software programs will do this for you, but why spend the money when a simple Excel file will do the job. Let's say you get paid every two weeks and, if married, so does your spouse. Your column headings should be the dates of your paydays, and you should prepare columns for every pay check for the next thirteen months, not twelve, so that you can see exactly what is coming in every pay period.

Then we go to the rows, starting with income. Let's say we have a newly married couple, Matt & Valerie. Matt has a regular job and Valerie works part-time, with both being paid twice a month on the 15th and 30th of the month. Our first rows should list every single line item of income, including any gifts received, bonuses, tax refunds, investment gains, etc. Don't worry I will give you an example in a few pages. The wages listed should be the actual amount deposited into your family checking account after taxes and deductions.

Our first row after income will be a budgeted amount every month for savings. Pay yourself before you consume. The psychological reason we list it first is that by listing it first we understand the importance of savings, and it is hard to reduce that amount if it is first. Use Quicken or Mint software to provide your actual checking numbers and pay everything through that account while categorizing it by income or expense category.

Our next set of rows should be for the cost of housing. List everything on its own row: rent/mortgage payment; heat; electric; water; sewer; internet; cable; insurance; repairs; dues; fees; property taxes if you have them; home repairs; security; and anything else you may have. List these expenses under the nearest due date column, but always for the pay period before the due date-we want to build good credit here too.

The next set of rows will be for transportation costs, by row. Start with car payments; insurance; licenses; repairs; gas and anything else that comes to mind.

The next set of rows will be for personal items in your order of importance. Start with food; followed by charity; medical, cell phones; eating out; furniture; clothes; gifts; school; kids; installment loans; credit cards; and everything else on which you spend money. If you are saving for a house down payment add a separate special line for it as a monthly goal. At the bottom, we will total each column to identify pay period shortfalls/overages, and to accumulate totals.

Here is a sample of a few months of Matt & Valerie's Excel budget sheet.

Matt & Valerie Budget: Dec 2017-January 2019					
Cash In	12/15	12/30	1/15	1/30	2/15
Matt Wage	1400	1400	1400	1400	1400
Matt 2nd Job wage	250	250	250	250	250
Valerie Wage	300	300	300	300	300
Gifts Received		1000			
Federal tax refund					2500
State Tax Refund					300
Other					
Total Cash In	1950	2950	1950	1950	4750
Cash Out					
Savings	200	200	200	200	500
Household					
Mortgage (includes escrow)		1700		1700	
Electric	80		80		80
Heat	150		175		175
Water		30		30	
Sewer		30		30	
Trash					
Cable					
Insurance-in escrow for them					
RE Tax-in escrow					
Internet		70		70	
Home Repairs/Maint		200			200
Yard/Snow					
Security					
Other	50		50		50
Total Household	280	2030	305	1830	505
Transportation					
Car Pmt Matt					
Car Pmt Valerie	250		250		250
Insurance	60		60		60
Repairs/Maintenance	75				
Gas	20		20		20
License					
Other					
Total Transportation	405	0	330	0	330
Other					
Food	300	300	300	300	300
Charity		100		100	
Medical	100		100		100
Entertainment		100		100	
Cell phone		50		50	
Clothes	50		50		50
School					
Student Loan Pmt					
Furniture Pmt					
Gifts		250			
Other					
Other					
Other					
Total Other Expenses	450	800	450	550	450
Total Cash Out	1335	3030	1285	2580	1785
Paycheck Difference	615	-80	665	-630	2965
Running Difference	795	715	1380	750	3715

So, what do Matt & Valerie do with this budget? First make it as accurate and realistic as possible for both cash in and cash out. Don't fudge any amounts, be realistic or it doesn't do any good. Then establish some goals: credit card payoffs; installment loan payoffs; car loan payoffs; savings for college; savings for safety, etc.

The next step is to go back through and see where the fat can be cut. Be realistic here, you still will go out to eat occasionally, there will be unexpected expenses (particularly when you have kids or medical issues) and allow yourself a bit of leeway. I like seeing 5% minimum to savings every month, and you may want to change the charity based on your personal beliefs. When looking to cut back, start with easy steps like cutting out one cup of store-bought coffee for each of you, every month, or one other personal vice such as alcohol, cigarettes, donuts, etc.!

Several years ago, I had a newly married young couple come in my office: Cassie and Steve. Their parents had sent them to see me because they never had any money, were expecting a child, and had high expectations of what life would give them. Cassie was a secretary in a law firm and Steve was a body shop manager, both good jobs.

They each drove up separately in new cars and walked in carrying a cup of Starbucks. After introductions, I asked what their long-term goals were. They both said they would like to retire in their fifties to travel, and that they would like a second home in Florida. Well, these are nice goals and certainly reasonable goals and I learned early in my career not to make judgments. However, I also know why their parents sent them to me-someone needed to open their eyes to realism.

There is no easy way to break it to them, so I threw it right out. Cassie had a good job, as did Steve, but they had absolutely zero chance of reaching those goals in their current jobs and consumption levels. Cassie and Steve had two options: either get a different job with more upward mobility; or lower what they were spending, because except for inflation they would never make any more than what they were now making, and by spending everything they earned just to get by it meant they would never reach any goals, or security or savings.

Not all my stories have a good ending because Cassie said no one had ever spoken to her like that and stormed out. Steve was kind of apologetic and was starting out the door when I said to him, "Steve just consider what I said since no one wants to hear bad news". The good news is a couple of years later I heard through their folks that they were embarrassed but would like to come back in and talk, which we did, and we have continued a thirty-five-year relationship. Two years ago, they had their oldest son, graduating from college, come in and get "the talk".

The next thing to do with this detailed budget is to prepare a more general five-year budget. It does not have to be by pay period, it can be by month, but it needs to include rows for your goals of savings, investment or whatever. If you have a goal of paying something off highlight that month's box for the emotional satisfaction!

The last thing to do with the budget is to sit down after the first month (together if two of you) and go through what worked, where you failed, and to adjust for the future. Keep a copy of the budget for the future because it will be interesting in ten or fifteen years to see how far you have come! Then, have a periodic "board" meeting over dinner, and go over the budget's past and the adjustments for the future. ***Frankly, a budget is the key to your financial success and the single best piece of advice in this entire book!***

So now that we know how to start saving, the next question is where should we put it? I would start with a simple account at the same local bank that you either have your mortgage with, or wish you had your mortgage with! It is time to work on relationships, and the first step is to develop a banking relationship for the long-term. Make sure your checking, and savings, and yes, mortgage are at the same bank. I know all the experts tell you to open an investment account online. Folks, that will come down the road, but for now we need some local relationships and the investment returns will not matter for a few years when the amounts involved are counted in hundreds of dollars, or a few thousand dollars. The type of account is not too important either at the beginning, we are not talking about returns in the hundreds of dollars. Get a reasonable return on a money market or savings account, but avoid the CD (Certificate of Deposit) for now.

Open an account at that local bank and if possible, direct deposit 5% from your paycheck to that account. Here is a point on the savings account: do not get a debit card or setup online access for now. Until you develop the ability to leave the account untouched, this account needs to be hard to access because the temptation to use it is too strong, particularly when you first start. This advice flies in the face of conventional wisdom, and frankly that's one of the reasons for this book. Conventional wisdom does not have forty years of experience with 10,000 tax returns, this book is based on the real-life observations of forty years and 10,000 returns. Open the local account and avoid easy access.

If you are particularly concerned, when you open the account require both signatures to make a withdrawal! That's a tough one, but it does assure that a decision to withdraw is a joint decision. However, in the event of an emergency the money would not be easily accessible, so I generally advise against the dual signature requirement.

Let's go back to Matt & Valerie for a minute. Notice that the bottom right number of $3,715 is their running excess of cash coming in. They need to leave around $1,000 in that checking account at all times (remember the bank relationship here) to allow for fluctuations and emergencies, but anytime that balance exceeds $1,000, transfer a nice round excess amount to the savings account. In Matt & Valerie's case I would transfer $2,500 to savings, leaving the $1,215 in checking for next pay period.

Once that savings account hits $10,000 it's time to go to the next chapter. Before we go there let's talk for a minute about that issue I raised earlier, bank relationships. In business, particularly local and small business, the relationship is based on one thing:

character. The character thing has been around in banking (and small business) forever, and historically was part of the "3 c's" lenders used to evaluate a customer. (Character, credit and collateral) It is still part of the equation today, even though it may not be in writing, and most bankers (and small business men and women) will determine some things, maybe incorrectly, about you based on the way you act.

When I used to hire regularly I would take a prospective employee to a local restaurant and see how they interacted with the waiters, service personnel and other people in the restaurant. I would try to get them excited about a sports team's opponents to see how they spoke. I learned long ago to determine whether I wanted to be involved in a business relationship based upon how the individual interacted with service personnel at a restaurant. If they treated the waiter/waitress and busboys with courtesy and respect, I was interested in working further. Without a "please", a "thank-you" or some other acknowledgment it was evident they had no respect for the service person. To go a step further, as a prospective employer I did not want anyone to think they were too good for any job, and this treatment of a service person gave me the impression I needed. In our office, I will never ask someone to do something because I do not want to do it, and that includes cleaning the restrooms. Ask my office.

I also listened to the way they spoke. I am not a believer in the theory that people who curse lack education or vocabulary. I am a complete believer in the theory that people who curse lack respect for the people they are with, as are most business folks. Curse words may be fine in your line of thinking, that's your call, but cursing in front of (or online) someone with whom you want to develop a business relationship has already shown your lack of respect for them, and some words in particular (you know them) cross a line that is difficult to cross back. If you want to develop a business relationship, treat people courteously in both your actions and your words.

3
SAVING MID-LIFE

This chapter requires that you have $10,000 in a bank savings account safety fund before you begin reading. Seriously. If you don't have $10,000, go back and read chapter two and accumulate $10,000 before worrying about other savings ideas. Once you have $10,000 sitting safely in the account at your local bank, where you have peace of mind, access and a good banking relationship, make sure to introduce yourself to the local bank manager to continually improve the relationship you have built, making sure in a quiet manner to emphasize your long-term relationship goals with the bank. You may never need the help, but there is no downside to having a local bank manager on your side, backed up by a checking, savings and possibly mortgage loan with a good history of timely payments and no overdrafts. Let me emphasize the overdraft issue in one simple summary: Don't ever do it. Mistakes will happen, I know I have had two or three in forty years, but the bank will overlook the rare mistakes. They will not overlook regular occurrences.

Let's move forward. You have accumulated the safety fund, what's next? Start by not quitting. Continue to budget and follow the budget, continue to save your change if you are doing so, continue to deposit 5% of every check in a savings tool as discussed below, and then look at some alternatives.

Begin step two in your savings plan by setting a goal or two for the extra money. Is your goal early or supplemental retirement? Is it a bigger home or kid's college? Is it investment property to generate more income? Set a couple of goals and determine what amount you would like to have to achieve that goal, and then change the savings account line item(s) in your budget. You may have to change the title of your existing 5% budget row to accommodate the breakdown of your goals into one amount of 3% of pay for goal one, and one amount of 2% of pay for goal two, or whatever works for you, and list those items as line items in your budget worksheet so that you psychologically know what you are saving for. Goals work, and it is important to list, quantify and measure progress towards those goals with a budget.

In the early 1980's a new financial certification program began in America, called the Certified Financial Planner (CFP®). I examined the program and was so interested in the things I would learn about insurance, investments, estates, trusts and planning in general that I signed up for the very difficult program of study and series of (at that time) six individual exams. As a Certified Public Accountant (CPA) I had detailed knowledge of accounting, preparing financial statements and performing audits; and rudimentary knowledge of income tax, legal and business issues, but no professional training whatsoever in the science of investments. This program would help fill those voids. Let me state that clearly: a tax advisor (CPA, EA or other) has had no formal investment training to be licensed as a tax preparer. I can say this with authority because I am a currently licensed Indiana CPA, and a IRS enrolled agent (EA) and any other tax license you want-there is no training here for investments or investment advising.

The training I received in studying for the CFP® exams was the single most useful and practical training I ever received in any topic. At the time I passed the exams in the early 1980's and became certified, I was alone in my state as a CPA/CFP®, and even though I have let my CFP® license expire through retirement, I still recognize it as a mark of knowledge and professionalism. I do not receive any commission, referral or free products from any person, company or society regarding this advice, I just want to protect you, the reader, through good advice.

I bring the discussion of the CFP® up because there are so many "investment advisors" marketing their services. The majority of these advisors are trained in sales or specific products, not investment concepts, by their underlying broker or dealer. They have had to pass a series of exams from the SEC to sell the products, but the studying for the licensing exam tests is not knowledge of investment advising. I used to have all those SEC licenses myself, and frankly the exams were a joke compared to the CFP® and CPA exams. SEC licenses by themselves are not an indicator of any advisory knowledge. Of course, knowledgeable advisors may exist without having CFP® after their name, but how do you know? If you are looking for outside advice, this seems to be the safest approach, looking for a CFP® who charges a small percentage of assets under management to manage your money, not one who sells you commission-based mutual funds and products.

But do you really need the services of an investment advisor? This I cannot say, but I do know that most of the major mutual fund families (Vanguard is my favorite, and my investment family of choice for my own investments) offer an incredible array of investment tools at little or no charge and provide professional guidance about investment choices within their mutual fund family. Simply putting your money in a calendar year based mutual fund often performs as well as any other investment program. What is a" calendar year based mutual fund"? Let's say you want to retire at age 60, which coincides for you with the calendar year 2040. You would invest in a "2040" fund through your mutual fund company, and the fund would invest in age appropriate items for you, with a heavy weight towards stock for younger Americans, moving away from stock to utility companies as you age and then to fixed income things such as bonds and preferred stocks as you age.

This is not an investment book, but a key concept in investment choices is to take greater risks earlier in life and lesser risks as you age, because early in life investment mistakes can be overcome, but late in life investment mistakes cannot. So, an investment for a twenty-something should be greatly weighted towards aggressive stocks, while investments for a sixty-something should be greatly weighted to fixed income, lower risk investments such as utilities and preferred stocks. Of course, this choice should be modified based on your personal acceptance or aversion to risk.

What about making your own investment choices? Wellllll, how good are you in reading financial statements, digging through the footnotes, understanding BETA and P/E ratios and looking at future trends? Just as I thought.

One of the best things I ever learned from my Dad was to not gamble on things I did not understand, and before participating, learning how to both make money *and lose money.* One of the best lessons he gave me early in life was teaching me how to play poker by computing odds and counting cards, and then telling me I had no business ever playing poker. When I asked him why, he said I understood how to make money because he had never met anyone who could remember every card played and calculate the odds on the remaining cards, but that I did not know how to lose money playing poker. I can still remember saying "But Dad, I know every card that has been played, and I know the probability of every card coming" and his response was one of those life lessons we all need when he said "Bobby, your face tells me what you know-you have the worst poker face I have ever seen". In other words, until I knew how to lose money playing poker I had no business playing poker. To this day, I won't play poker, although I have been known to count a few Blackjack cards!

Here is a simple test: do you know what a DRIP is? do you know how often dividends are paid? do you know the two primary ways to make money on a stock? If you cannot correctly answer all three questions you have no business buying individual stocks because you don't have enough knowledge to understand how you make *and lose* money investing in the stock market. Let me give you some basic guidance please.

There are two primary ways to make money on a stock investment; a return of annual profits to you in cash (called a dividend) normally paid every three months; and an increase in the underlying value of the stock on the stock market. For example, historically AT&T has paid a very good dividend of about 5-6% annually and is considered a blue-chip stock. If you bought 100 shares of AT&T at $40 per share you would have invested $4,000 in AT&T. The dividend for the year would be about $240, paid in four quarterly payments of $60 each. If at the end of the year AT&T was now selling at $42 per share you would have made $2x100=$200 on the underlying stock price increase and $240 in dividends for a total return of $440 for the year, or an 11% return. (440/4000). Of course, a stock price may go down as well, and dividends may be cut, although a dividend cut very rarely occurs in blue chip stocks.

If you decide to go ahead and invest in the stock market directly by buying an individual stock, please avoid the pot of gold syndrome. This is a term I use for people that think they will find the pot of gold at the end of the rainbow, or in a stock market analogy invest in something believing they will get rich overnight. It won't happen. After forty years and 10,000 clients I have never, ever seen someone get rich on an individual stock investment, except in their own company. They may have made a profit, even excellent profits, but I have never seen a pot of gold. Buying stock should only be done after reading about the company, observing analyst's opinions and evaluating your own ideas of risk and return. You do not have to be able to understand everything in a financial statement, just basic terms, but you do need to read the analyst opinions from several advisors.

I cannot advise you on your own levels of risk, but I will tell you that if you are hoping for an average return exceeding 8-10% annually over many years, then you are not being realistic. To achieve a return that exceeds those historically maximum averages, the risk exceeds the chance of succeeding. If an investment advisor suggests that he or she can earn more than these averages in your account, run, run away unless you understand the incredible risks you are taking with a minimal chance of getting a higher return. In other words, an investment advisor promising returns exceeding this common-sense limit are usually either ignorant of historical market risk/return rates or are motivated by their commissions more than reality. In particular, avoid advisors claiming they have a "system". Steve Wynn, the founder of the Las Vegas Mirage casino always said he would send a plane for you if you had a "system"!

You invest in the stock market by opening an account online with one of the major online brokerage companies like Schwab, Fidelity, Ameritrade, etc., and transferring money into it electronically from your existing bank, or with a check. You can also have money withheld from your paycheck for ongoing investments with most brokerage companies. Once the account is open you put in a "buy" order using a company's stock abbreviation (called a stock symbol), and listing the number of shares you want to buy, and how you want to buy them: market price or limit price. Once you open an account, you do not have to buy anything of course, as you may wish to just use it as a second, interest-earning account. An advantage in opening an account with Schwab or Fidelity or the bigger brokers is free access to investment analysts; those people who analyze individual companies. A common mistake is to open accounts with multiple brokers. Use just one account to keep life simple. I personally use Fidelity because of the access to nearly anything I want to use, plus analyst's opinions, but any of the major brokers are just fine.

Here are some consistently bad choices for making investments, in order, for the worst choices:

1. Penny stocks,
2. Stock "tips",
3. Friends,
4. TV ads,
5. Commissioned sales people.

In other words, I am not a fan of individual stock investments for most people, including myself. You can really hit it big if you choose the right one, but the most common outcome is to not hit it big because the source of information is bad. Penny stocks are notorious for fraud; stock "tips" are the worst possible way to make an investment; guidance from friends: are they trained in investments and have they read the financial statements in depth? TV ads are used when no one else will sell the product; and commissioned sales people are motivated to sell you something they make a lot of money selling, not what you need. Let me tell you two stories from the past in my office.

Gerald inherited a large dollar amount of stock in four or five major companies from his father. The stocks were known as blue chip stocks, which means they were large, stable, multi-national companies with good dividend rates. Dividends are checks paid quarterly to stockholders, much like interest on a savings account. Blue chip companies have a long history of paying slowly increasing dividends. Gerald immediately signed up to have ½ of the dividends reinvested in the individual companies through the company's dividend reinvestment programs (or DRIP). The DRIP allows the stockholder to buy more stock with the quarterly dividend, often at a discount and with minimal commission, and is often an excellent benefit to look for as an investor. You will sometimes hear an investment advisor say that it would be cheaper buying the stock directly, which is often technically correct, but *for a small investor that does not have the extra money* to buy more stock directly, a DRIP is an excellent tool.

Over the next thirty years Gerald watched the companies closely by reading their annual reports, watching what investment analysts had to say about the specific companies, watching (and reinvesting ½) the dividends, and occasionally buying or selling some of the shares. He never actively traded the shares or modified his holdings much. The re-invested dividends over thirty years, combined with the underlying growth in the value of the stock meant that after thirty years the value of his holdings provided him with substantial annual income that increased every year as dividends increased, and left him a sizable portfolio even until his death, which passed on to his daughter.

She still follows her Dad's advice now, six years after his death, and has provided for both of her sons' college, even though her knucklehead husband has *income tax blindness* and "invests" all his money in Alpacas (seriously). She won't let her husband touch the money she inherited because her common-sense answer was that her Dad did very well on his investments, how were the Alpacas working out for him? (Here is a hint-every tax advisor in America laughs at the clients that invest in Alpacas, Llamas or most horses-all historically *income tax blindness* investments that are known by tax advisors as pot of gold money pits).

Before we discuss the second example let's talk about DRIP's for a moment. I love them and strongly recommend using them, particularly for kid's investments. When my son was born over thirty years ago, my wife and I invested $100 in Coca Cola for him because it was a blue-chip stock, with a 3% (at the time) annual dividend and a DRIP. We recognized that a 3% annual dividend meant that he would receive four checks during the year of $.75 each ($3 total return), which would not have any effect on anyone's life! We enrolled him in the DRIP, which continues to this day. As Coca Cola stock value grew, it split a couple of times, and continued to pay decent dividends. He now has over 125 shares of Coca Cola, valued at over $5,000 from that simple start thirty years ago. We made a similar $1,000 investment in the Vanguard Wellesley mutual fund, also telling them to reinvest all dividends (yes mutual funds may also offer the DRIP option), and today the value of that investment is a little over $32,000. Yes, I like DRIPs for the common-sense factor that a dividend check on a small investment will mean nothing when you get that tiny quarterly check, but by reinvesting that money over a long period of time the returns can be incredible. Here is an excellent summary of available DRIPs from a DRIP trustee/agent: https://www.amstock.com/investpower/new_plandet2.asp Now back to the second story.

Gerald's sister Ruth inherited the exact same stockholdings when their father died forty years ago. Ruth did not like some of the investments because they were too conservative and immediately sold all of them, reinvesting in various much more aggressive stock investments, based on her own "research" which consisted of articles she had read in various magazines, TV shows, friends and ironically a broker trained in selling stock but not in investment plans.

When Gerald died about ten years ago, I did his estate tax return, so I knew the value of his stock holdings, and his sister Ruth passed away seven months later, also at an elderly age. Ironically, although Ruth had invested very aggressively, she had never found the "pot of gold". The value of her holdings, she was proud to say, was still as much as she received when her father had died thirty years prior. Of course, I was unable to speak about it, but her brother had pulled out nearly $900,000 in dividends over the years, and had seen the value of his investments grow by almost $2,000,000 (the DRIP's $900,000 in reinvested dividends, plus underlying stock price growth of $1.1 million). The moral of the story? Ruth had taken extreme risks for an actual lesser return than the blue chips over a long period of time. If you are a long-term investor, don't search for the pot of gold, invest in blue chips. Although an individual story, I have seen this result many times in 40 years.

Are your only mid-life investment choices individual advisors, or brokers, or your own stock investments? Of course not. You can buy mutual funds, which are a diversified group of investments with a specific investment strategy directly from a mutual fund company. Go to www.Vanguard.com for a good, low-cost mutual fund family.

Physical Assets

What about investing in gold, silver and similar hard assets? These historically high risk investments theoretically offer protection if everything else goes to pot, so I will limit this discussion to a few basics. My personal opinion is to buy silver, not gold if you invest in bullion, because silver has more commercial application and can much more easily be used as currency than a gold coin. At the time of this writing a gold eagle was worth about $1,600 and a silver eagle about $19. You buy the coins at a premium and the bars at a quoted price. I like the coins, and am willing to pay a premium because the coins would be immediately usable in a calamity, whereas bullion would have to be measured, weighed and cut. Yes, I do own some silver as a safety mechanism, stored in a safe deposit box, but it represents about 2% of my family's net worth. I cannot address any other hard asset investments such as art, jewelry and collectibles because they are specialized things that require specialized knowledge.

Real estate represents the third leg of a four-legged investment stool, after stocks and hard assets, with the fourth leg being private investments.

Real estate is a funny thing. In certain areas of the country it is a roller-coaster with levels of risk from the use of leveraging (borrowed money) offering returns in sky-high amounts. However, every ten to fifteen years the real estate market seems to go through a bust cycle (think 2007-2009) which destroys a lot of those risk-takers in these areas of the country. In other areas of the country real estate investments offer a stable rate of return in the form of rent and slow property value growth, much lower risk levels and an opportunity to have someone else (the tenant) share the risk. In a simplified manner, (ignoring REIT funds) real estate investments are direct investments by an individual in either residential rental properties or commercial properties, or some mix of the two. Almost all individual real estate investments involve a large percentage (20-30%) of the purchase price provided by debt, and many banks will not lend on residential rental, so do your homework.

Borrowing against your personal residence to buy a rental property is a miserable choice from both a risk as well as a tax deduction measurement point of view. You have bet your home against the value of the rental property, which in my mind is too great a risk to take. We have sadly seen many aggressive "advisors" tell people to borrow against their home equity to invest in real estate, and sadly the investors do not understand the risk they are taking. Do not risk your home for rental property. As stated in chapter one, the only time you should ever borrow against your home is to increase the value of the home itself, or to pay for your kid's college.

The tax deduction for interest on a rental home is excellent except when you borrow against your personal residence to buy the rental home, in which case the interest deduction is limited to the interest paid on $100,000 of debt. The loan needs to be against the rental property, not your personal residence to be able to deduct all the interest. You see, even Congress does not want you to risk your home to buy rental property! By the way, if your tax advisor says this is wrong, change tax advisors as they do not understand the acquisition debt vs. equity debt rules that I have discussed in our tax seminars for tax experts for several years.

At one time in the mid-1990's I owned, along with my two cousins, over thirty-five individual rental properties. They usually made a decent income, most of them made a little profit in the underlying property value, and they were all a royal pain in the backside because of deadbeat tenants, repairs, improvements, assessments, etc. Although we were not slumlords and always investigated tenants, we still saw dozens of bad tenants. One thing to note is that it is the rare tenant who has "pride of ownership", so the repairs are consistently more than you expect. Although the properties made money, in retrospect they weren't worth the hassle. It came to a head for me when I evicted four motorcycle gang members at the point of a shotgun, and we had checked the guy out signing the lease very carefully. That day we decided to sell all the properties.

Since that time, we (my cousins and I) have all individually re-invested in commercial property. We had no disagreements, we just chose to go it on our own now that we each had a little money of our own. The residential rental homes were bought with no money down because three of us had individually guaranteed the loan. Don't get me wrong, there is money to be made in residential rental, but you had better be willing to do as much repair, maintenance and management as you can to maximize the profit. If you pay a property manager most profits will evaporate unless the property has minimal debt.

Commercial property enjoys long-term leases that are much more commonly followed and more easily enforced and can also offer potential for underlying property value increases, all with less management issues than other property. Commercial tenants often have "pride of ownership" because it has a direct relationship to sales and profitability of their business. Having been a commercial property owner for about twenty years now, I find it much more pleasant, with much fewer headaches and similar, if not greater returns. The restriction on commercial property is that it does take some up-front cash.

Should you join with someone else in a partnership or LLC to buy real estate? That question is right up there with "Should I get married?". A partnership is a legal marriage, and my advice is to be very, very, very careful with whom you do this. With my cousins and I we had all grown up together, trusted each other implicitly, and trusted the responsibility that each showed. Would I do it again with them? Yes. Would I enter a real estate partnership with someone else? That would require some pretty deep thought, a written allocation of management responsibilities, goals and decision making, and most importantly a "divorce clause" for how to get out if things didn't work. I like a divorce clause that says the party wanting out pays to get the property appraised, and then offers to either buy out the partner or sell to the partner at the appraised price times their ownership percentage.

Direct Investments in Businesses

Don't you wish Bill Gates had been your neighbor and asked you to be an early investor? Or what about Steve Jobs or Mark Zuckerburg? Yep, all three would have been excellent initial investments. How often do you think that happens in real life? Buy a lottery ticket, you've got a better chance!

Once you accumulate your $10,000 you may be offered an opportunity to invest in a family member, friend or mutual acquaintance's business. You won't hear me tell you no. You will hear me tell you to be cautious. Here is the first question to ask yourself: Can you recover if you lose everything you invest? If the answer is yes, then let's ask some more questions. If the answer is no, you still won't hear me tell you not to do it, but if you are over age 50, I will very strongly suggest you can't take the risk. Once an individual hits age 50 I have always firmly believed they should not make any investment that could bankrupt them, because there is not enough time left in their life to recover. OK, enough pessimism, let's look at some things to consider.

First, is the investment an ownership position or a loan? If it is a loan then draw up a loan document, with payment terms, interest and collateral. If it is an investment, get it in writing and when you hand over the money you should get a stock certificate or ownership paper, legally signed and transferred. Don't put the money in however, until you ask the rest of the questions below, but be clear going in what you are being asked for. Ownership positions have a greater possibility of a good return than loans, but both are similar, extremely high-risk transactions, so I would go for ownership.

Second, ask some common-sense business questions such as who is your customer, what will be the price of your product or service, how will you market it, what is your budget, who will work the concept and how much, and the number one question of all, what is your break-even point?

We had a new tenant in our office building a few years ago that sold a service to the general public. Their rent was exactly $2,200 monthly (which included utilities) and by coincidence they were charging $22 for each service. They were only open weekends (3 nights a week). One day I met her in the entryway and casually asked if she had gotten her needed 25 customers the previous weekend. She looked at me in total confusion and said, and I quote, "What?". I casually explained that since she needed to earn $2,200 every month to pay her rent and she charged $22 per person, that she needed 100 customers in a month, and since she was open 4 weekends a month, that it worked out to 25 people per weekend or 8 people daily. Her response was not new to me and illustrates a basic failing point in many small businesses. Her break-even point is the number of customer service or item sales she needs to make at her sales price to provide enough money to cover the costs of operations, yet she had opened her business without knowing how many customers were going to be needed just to pay the bills.

In my experience if a new business does not know what their break-even point is just to pay its expenses, then the business concept is so poorly thought out that it runs a 90-100% chance of failure. What do you mean by "your experience"? That would be the 2,000-3,000 small business ideas that have run across my desk in the last 40 years. This tenant went out of business at the end of their lease.

A well-thought out new business will have a business plan illustrating who the target customers are, how they will be persuaded to buy the service or product (marketing), a short and long term budget (sound familiar?) with sales goals, and financial projections showing sales projections with various levels of sales, and most importantly, the minimum amount needed to "break-even".

In summary, before you invest in a friend/family business ask for a copy of their business plan and what their break-even point is. No plan? No investment. Ask them to prepare a plan with financials and come back showing you how they will make enough money to first break-even, and second make a profit. The lack of a plan does not necessarily mean the business won't be successful, but it does illustrate poor planning which leads to a lack of success.

You have worked hard for your money, and to lose it by investing in a poorly planned small business idea is just as bad as losing it to Bernie Madoff. Please follow this advice.

Does this mean all new small businesses are bad ideas? Of course not, here are some more stories from my CPA firm history book.

Early in my career I had a good friend, and client, that was a well-respected foreign car mechanic. One day he called for an appointment and came by to talk. He had just realized that his earnings as a W-2 employee at the dealership were at the highest level they would ever be, and he asked what his options were. As a friend, I told him that unless he changed careers, this was correct. He surprised me when he said he had come to the same conclusion and was thinking about opening his own auto repair shop. He surprised me even further when he said he had spent the last weekend at local shopping malls putting flyers under the windshields of every car in the lot made by the manufacturer of his specialty. This is a business plan my friends! He proceeded to open an unbelievably successful auto repair shop.

Several years later this same friend and client approached me to invest in a new franchise auto oil-change business as an owner. He had a written plan and wanted help in determining whether the idea would work. It did, I did, and it was one of the best investments I ever made.

The second story involves a real estate broker and client/friend who wanted to develop some land into a subdivision. His preparation was impeccable, his financials and plans were excellent and he was a real estate expert. He also needed financial backing and once again I participated and the results were excellent.

So, what is the similarity in the two real-life stories? In both cases the businesses were being built by knowledgeable people, who knew how to make *and lose* money in the business, had a well-thought out business plan, and prepared financial projections. Of course, these factors do not guarantee the success of the business, but they are indicators of the probability of success and are factors you should look for when thinking of investing in a small business.

4
SAVING AT 55 AND OLDER

Saving at age 55 or older requires a different outlook than we have previously discussed. The outlook can be summarized with three "S"'s. Safety, security and simplicity.

At age 55 the average person has about thirty years left in their life according to the Social Security administration's life expectancy estimates, or about 1/3 of their total life span. During the first one-third of their life their activities may be characterized as learning, reproducing and building for the next two-thirds of their and their offspring's life. This period of life is characterized by high energy, high hopes and high achievement in the terms of financial activity tied to consumption. Financially this period is characterized by high debt, growing earnings levels, high spending and little accumulation.

The second one-third of the average American's life represents a changeover to a frame of mind involving building a strong and secure future for themselves and their offspring. This period is also characterized by good, but slowly declining health; a tempering of hopes to more realistic views of future accomplishments; and a realization of impending, but distant mortality. This section of life represents, for the wiser individual, debt reduction, asset accumulation (often just in retirement plans), and a peak in annual earnings.

The final one-third of life is divided into two or three distinct periods: a final burst of income-producing work activity to accumulate assets towards the remaining time left; a mid-session of activity after retirement while health issues grow and activity diminishes; and a final maintenance period prior to death where health, energy and activity levels rapidly decline and assets are rapidly diminished. During this period, the accumulation of assets for retirement becomes a primary goal at the beginning, earnings are steady at first and then quickly diminish, and asset conservation becomes the number one concern around age seventy to seventy-five.

Chapter two was devoted to the first one-third period of your life; chapter three to the second one-third and this chapter to the final one-third. This chapter began with the introduction of the three "S"'s of safety, security and simplicity, three closely integrated goals during this period of life.

Safety

Safety in our discussion refers to the conscious decision to avoid any risk-based activity, particularly after retirement. This period of life represents a complete change of mind in thinking, from income-based *consumption* spending while working to asset-based *retention* spending during retirement. Sadly, over the years I have seen hundreds of clients fail to change their way of thinking from *consumption* to *retention* and continue consuming as they near or reach retirement. *Consuming* as retirement nears does not refer to food, clothing or medical costs, instead it refers to transferring income-earning, retirement oriented assets to non-incoming earning assets (and even value-declining things) such as home upgrades rather than home maintenance or down-sizing; new cars when the old ones are only a few years old; and similar activities. This book is written for the average American who needs to make do with what they have accumulated, not the wealthy with alternate sources of income or assets.

Recognizing that the ability to earn income diminishes rapidly at retirement, the financial mistakes made in youth must be avoided in this final one-third stage of life because income will no longer replace lost assets. This does not mean avoiding consumption, it means thoughtful decision making on purchases, investments and financial action. It means avoidance of any new debt incurrence, rapid elimination of existing debt (remember "Paid For" at 65), and aggressive retirement savings during the last flurry of work activity.

Because income will become fixed at retirement, a detailed, careful budget should be developed again at age 55 (many people will have dropped budgeting) with a primary goal of accumulating enough money at retirement to maintain the desired lifestyle as well as pay for increasing medical expenses.

So as far as safety goes, our summary is to continue to use and follow a budget, accumulate retirement funds as rapidly as possible during your last work years, eliminate all debt, and avoid financial decisions that incur risk, add to debt, or reduce your retirement savings. I would very strongly recommend reading the retirement and social security chapters as well.

Security

The second piece of our three-part strategy at age 55 is security. This discussion refers to safeguarding existing assets. Let's make it clear, for most Americans whatever you have accumulated by age 65 or so is all you will ever have, and it will slowly be reduced over the remainder of your life. Our security discussion begins with a quick review of investments, proceeds to internet security, and concludes with a discussion of reverse mortgages.

For those folks who are using investment advisors or mutual fund managers make sure you schedule a meeting with your advisor on your 55th birthday to discuss changes in your long-term investment strategy. The strategy late in life should involve the four concepts of very low risk holdings; with good dividends or interest payments; liquidity (the ability to rapidly convert to cash); and protection from inflation. I will defer to the opinion of your investment advisor, but often these holdings later in life are focused on utility and preferred stocks, REIT's, and bonds, all of which are watched closely for inflationary concerns. This strategy at age 55 would apply to both retirement money and any outside investments you hold.

If you are managing your own money, a similar outlook is appropriate. Low risk; income; liquidity; and inflation consciousness would apply to you as well. Again, these concepts apply to retirement accounts as well as any outside investments you may have. In general, if you own real estate, this is a relatively good investment in late life to address three of the four concerns I just mentioned, but bring their own headaches of management that must be considered during late life. Of course, the liquidity of real estate is poor and must be concerned in your overall retirement plan.

One of the most popular courses we teach to tax advisors is our security class, which is written and taught by myself and our company's IT director, Ryan Jennings (my son), who brings the current knowledge of internet issues to the course. Because one of the three most common sources of identity theft in our country is Americans over age 65, we can provide you with practical, yet easy guidance to protect you from an increasingly electronic society. Again, we do not receive commissions, referrals or free products from anyone, so you receive unbiased advice.

Let's begin with computer protection. Today, right now, download and install "Bit Defender", which is our recommended security suite software for the last several years. If you are relying on free anti-virus, outdated software or nothing then you are fooling yourself. An anti-virus software without other security features, particularly a free one, is the equivalent to rolling up your car windows in a high crime area while leaving the keys in the ignition! Bit Defender will cost about $50-60 for a three-year license.

Second, consider your own activity or the activity for which your computer is used. We have used a "no-click" policy at home and in our office for several years. This means we will not click on any links or attachments to any email without independent verification of the contents. Your number one electronic risk is clicking on a fraudulent email attachment and the simple solution is to follow our no-click policy.

The other thing you must change is a little touchier. The number one identity theft risk in America is individuals under age 18, and the number two risk is individuals from 18-22 years old. These age groups are at a high risk for identity theft because they engage in high-risk activities, take no precautions and do not believe anything can happen to them. Do not allow them to destroy your life electronically so today, right now, immediately, do not let anyone else use your computer, even if you trust them implicitly. Unless your grand child is an IT person they should not be allowed to use your computer, take it to the Geek Squad and get it updated and cleaned, or call a computer person to come to your house. At the same time, make sure your own "Wi-Fi" is secure by having the same IT person or Geek Squad set it up and tell them you want it set for high security.

Our final computer suggestions are basic. Always turn your computer off unless you are sitting in front of it, require a log-in password to start the system, and never provide your Social Security number online to anyone. The final recommendation is also hard to understand but must be followed. Never, ever, ever use free public "Wi-Fi". You are broadcasting your electronic information to everyone when you do this. On many occasions in our live Technology classes our IT Director will illustrate this by showing on the projector screen the names of everyone in the room using the facility's free "Wi-Fi", and if challenged or allowed, will take over the computer unobtrusively of anyone on a free system.

Reverse Mortgages

Reverse mortgages, (aka: Home Equity Conversion Mortgage (HECM)) which allow senior homeowners to convert home equity to cash, are steadily growing in popularity. The basic premise is that a homeowner may borrow equity out of his or her home without being required to make payments until they no longer live in the home. The amount that can be borrowed is a factor of the borrower's age (minimum age is 62), the current market interest rates, the home's value, and the amount of any current mortgage on the home. Generally, the older the borrower, the lower the current interest rate, and the higher the value of the home, the greater the amount that may be borrowed. Regardless of circumstances, most lenders have an overall maximum loan amount (i.e., FHA reverse mortgage maximum is $625,500).

Hint: You know an actor's career is over when he or she is selling reverse mortgages!

Reverse mortgages are available only to folks that are age 62 or older, who occupy the home as their principal residence with adequate equity, and who are not delinquent on any federal debt like an FHA loan. The number one complaint about home mortgages is the acceleration clause that exists in nearly all reverse home mortgages that requires full repayment within 30 days if the home is not occupied by the borrower, for any reason, for 12 months or more.

Reverse mortgages come in many variations, including:

a. Tenure - equal monthly payments if at least one borrower lives and continues to occupy the property as a principal residence.

b. Term - equal monthly payments for a fixed period of months determined at the outset of the loan.

c. Line of credit - unscheduled payments or installments are made to the borrower at times and in an amount of the borrower's choosing until the line of credit is exhausted.

d. Modified tenure - combination of a line of credit plus scheduled monthly payments for if borrower remains in the home.

e. Modified term - combination of line of credit plus monthly payments for a fixed period of months selected by the borrower.

f. Payment relief - allows borrower to stop making house payments on existing mortgage, even though there is not enough equity to allow for additional cash to be withdrawn.

Unlike ordinary home equity loans, borrowers do not make any payments on the reverse mortgage *if the home is the principal residence of the borrower.* Lenders recover their principal and interest when the borrower sells the home, dies, permanently moves to a new residence, or are absent from the home for a period of 12 months or more (i.e., move into long term care). Most lenders put into the loan agreement that the loan can be called in the event the borrower does not pay insurance or property taxes, or if the home is neglected and allowed to deteriorate. Any home equity remaining after the lender is paid all principal and interest on the mortgage belongs to the borrower or the borrower's estate.

Practical Note: Look at that *"absent from the home for a period of 12 months or more"* clause. If you die, can your kids pay off the loan within 30 days? If you go into a nursing home can you pay the loan off in 30 days? This clause is heavily abused and the ***US Consumer Fraud Bureau cites the high cost, heavy levels of fraud and high incidence of foreclosure after 30 days as major concerns. We are not proponents of reverse mortgages because of these abuses.***

Reverse mortgages and fees. The second biggest complaint about reverse mortgages are the fees, which typically are much greater than those associated with traditional mortgages. A borrower who obtains an FHA reverse mortgage would be required to pay:

- An origination fee of up to $6,000 ($2,500 for homes with values less than $125,000);
- Initial up front mortgage insurance premium (MIP) of .5% to 2.5% of the loan amount;
- Annual MIP of 1.25% of the outstanding loan balance; and
- A monthly loan servicing fee of up to $35 ($30 for fixed rate loans).
- Title and escrow fees needed to close the loan.

Example: Marge is 74 years old and owns her home free and clear. Marge decides she would like a little more monthly cash flow and is contemplating a reverse mortgage of $250,000. An FHA lender tells Marge it will cost her $10,750 of fees to obtain the reverse mortgage. The fees are calculated:

Origination fee (2% on first $200,000, 1% on balance)	$ 4,500
Initial MIP (2.5% of loan amount)	6,250
Closing costs, title and escrow (approximately ½%)	1,250
Total up-front costs	$12,000

Marge will also incur monthly service fee of $30 plus a monthly MIP fee of $1,250.

Practical Note: Fees such as above are typically added to the loan balance rather than requiring the borrower to spend cash to obtain the loan.

Simplicity

One of the more common concerns that I encounter as a professional is the taxpayer that has invested money in twenty or thirty different accounts, brokerage houses, banks, etc. Do you realize how complicated this makes things for yourself, for your caregivers and for your heirs? Most of the time no one has thought of this, but take it from a professional: it is ridiculous, expensive, time-consuming and frustrating to maintain multiple accounts. Our goal is simplicity. Use one checking and savings account per family. Use one brokerage company for any investments outside of a retirement account. If you own stocks individually you can transfer them to the brokerage account without having to sell them. Use one retirement account per individual, or at least combine them into just one brokerage company. Before transferring anything make sure to speak with your tax advisor, your retirement plan company and your investment advisor if you have one because occasionally we may be talking about a "rollover" or some other special situation, but simplicity is the goal.

The unspoken argument for simplicity is aging. What do you mean by that, Bob? As most people age I see them worry and incur great stress over keeping track of multiple accounts. I see their mental faculties slowly decline and then mistakes occur, causing more stress. I see people who are unfamiliar with investments before retirement struggling to make a complicated situation understandable after retirement, as their ability to understand the activities also declines. I see inexperienced spouses left to try to figure out what to do with ten different accounts in eight different institutions. And after forty years I have figured out a solution to this mess: simplicity.

Many years ago, I realized that my wife would likely outlive me. The men in my family tree all died in their fifties and early sixties for the most part, and I have had three different types of cancer as well as open heart surgery, combined with an aggressive Type A, heart-attack inducing personality. Knowing this, and as a beneficiary of an excellent marriage, I made sure to address simplicity early on, and after writing this chapter have sworn to carry it further. When we bought our home, we titled it solely in my wife's name, and did the same with a small second home in Florida. Our office buildings are owned by an LLC composed 2/3 of my wife and 1/3 by my son's trust. Assuming I do kick off first, Jean will have no worries about real estate transfers, and she also owns most of our outside investments outright. I know, if she decides to leave me for George Clooney I am in trouble, but that is a risk I can live with! What is left? For me, because I have several retirement plans in three different institutions, I am going to try to consolidate them into one, as should be your goal. My wife has two or three retirement accounts as well, and we will be consolidating them into one for her too.

So, in the final trimester of your life think of safety, security and simplicity. Simplicity in financial activities, security in daily activities, and safety in investment activities.

5
INCOME TAX GUIDANCE

We all want to benefit from the “tax shelters” used by “the rich”. We want the secrets they use to avoid tax. Well let me give you a hint-there aren’t any! These are terms invented by writers to make the income tax code interesting. I prepare tax returns for several folks worth millions of dollars. They utilize fancy hedge funds and ownership investments that are common for wealthier Americans, and they do have more opportunities to invest than the average American, but the bottom line is the hedge funds don’t ever seem to get a better return than any other good investment portfolio and the ownership investments don’t generate any more tax deductions than they would if you or I invested in them. Occasionally I will see someone “out on the edge” who is taking some nutty tax advice proposed by a national CPA firm that eventually fails 8-10 years later in a collapse in tax court. These folks have the same *“income tax blindness”* that I spoke about in the first chapter.

Our current income tax rates are still below the historic average rates our country has used for the roughly 100-year history of the income tax system, as shown below with the historic rate chart from the National Taxpayer’s Union.

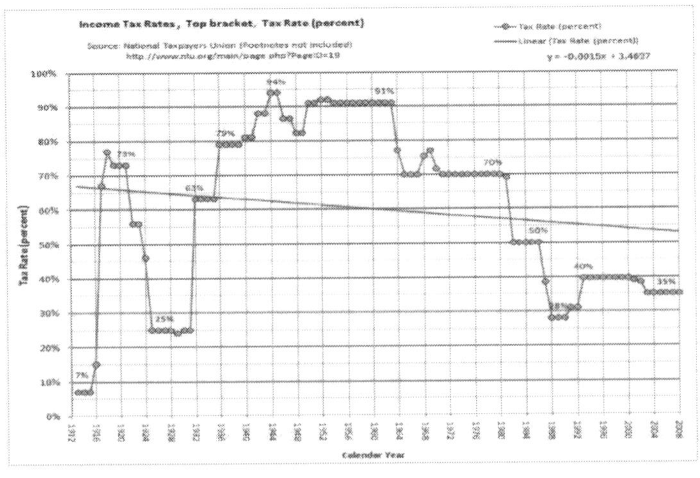

The fact that we continue to enjoy low rates doesn't mean that the average American cannot take advantage of Congressional rules allowing certain tax benefits. Remember, the only tax loopholes are those created by Congress when they write the tax law, and wealthy Americans follow the same rules as the rest of us. Average Americans have an advantage however, because there are a lot more tax benefits written for the average tax bracket American with a more generous net tax benefit than there are for wealthy Americans.

When I am preparing a tax return for an individual who complains about the income taxes they are paying the very first thing I examine is their W-2. You see, there are an incredible number of tax-free benefits available from Congress for W-2 employees, yet it is the very rare employee that utilizes them to their full advantage. The W-2 tells me what the employee is utilizing, and to what extent, as well as providing hints about may be overlooked by the employee.

Let's start by looking at the granddaddy of all tax shelters, the number one tool to use if it is available to you: the 401K and its sisters the 403B and 457 retirement plans. The GAO tells us that well over 60% of all working Americans are current participants in these plans. In layman's terms let's use a simple example. A 401K allows a W-2 worker to deposit money into the plan and only pay income tax on the net pay.

Example: Marion earns about $75,000 every year in her W-2 job at BigCorp. Her husband Ted makes nearly the same amount at a local employer. Both have 401K's available at work, but neither participates. Each may defer up to $18,000 (2017 amounts) every year to the 401K ($24,000 if they are over age 49!). Each employer also matches the first 3% of their W-2 contributed to the plan under current rules, plus 50% of the next 2% they put in. Let's see some summary numbers:

	Gross Pay	No contribution	Each put in 3% of pay	Each put in 5% of pay	Each put in maximum
Marion	75,000		2,250	3,750	18,000
Ted	75,000		2,250	3,750	18,000
Employer match	0	0	4,500	6,000	6,000
Total saved for retirement	**0**	**0**	**9,000**	**13,500**	**42,000**
Taxed family income	150,000	150,000	145,500	142,500	114,000
Income tax @20%	30,000	30,000	29,100	28,500	22,800
Cash left for the year after tax and 401K	120,000	120,000	116,400	114,000	91,200

Look at column 3-if Marion and Ted each put just 3% of pay into their 401K ($4,500 total), the magic of the 401K tax deferral means that it only cost them $3,600 in available cash (120,000-116,400) to get a total of $9,000 deposited into their retirement accounts. They have received an incredible, immediate, tax-deferred return of 150% return on their investment! (Their investment only cost them $3,600, but they received $9,000 in 401K deposits for a $5,400 increase (5400/3600 =150%). This is a risk-free return that cannot be matched and anyone working for an employer with a 401K that does not deposit at least 3% is an absolute fool.

What about column 4-if Marion and Ted each put just 5% of pay into their 401K ($7,500 total), the magic of the 401K tax deferral means that it only cost them $6,000 in available cash (120,000-114,000) to get a total of $13,500 deposited into their retirement accounts. Their investment cost them $6,000, but they received $13,500 in 401K deposits for a $7,500 increase, or a 125% immediate, risk-free and tax deferred return, again a deal that should never be turned down.

If Marion and Ted are serious about putting aside money for retirement they may defer as much as $18,000 each (2017 limit) to their 401K each year, increasing to $24,000 each year once they hit age 50. In their case, the last column shows that a total contribution of $36,000 ($18,000 each) only cost them $28,800 after tax (120,000-91,200), and that it enabled a whopping $42,000 contribution to their 401K's for this year. So, they received $42,000 in 401K deposits for a net cost of $28,800 or a $14,000 increase, which is about a 45% return on their investment. It doesn't get any better than this in America, and this beats any "tax shelter" or alternative investment available today. Show me any other risk-free investment that will earn you 45%, worst case-it doesn't exist my friends.

Over the years, I have had many clients complain about paying too much tax and commenting that they need a tax shelter or write-off, and I then see that they are not even fully participating in the best tax shelter of all in their own 401K. If Marion and Ted bring me their W-2's and Box 12 of their W-2 shows nothing contributed to a 401K, or any amount less than $18,000 contributed I will tell them that until they max out the 401K contribution there is no reason to look for tax shelters or even other investments because the 401K guarantees then an instant, risk-free 45% return! ***The number 1 tax shelter <u>AND INVESTMENT</u> available to Americans earning less than $150,000 annually is to deposit the maximum amount allowed to their 401K.***

Even self-employed individuals may set up and participate in 401K plans. For those people who work for an employer that does not sponsor a 401K plan, ask them to start one! If enough employees ask they may consider it as a low-cost fringe benefit. At my own company (TaxSpeaker) we offer a 401K through Vanguard. It costs the company about $4,000 annually for the plan, plus the employer contribution.

<u>Cafeteria Plans</u>

These plans go by many names but all have the same characteristics. Common names for cafeteria plans include Section 125 plans, 125 plans, flex plans, flex spending accounts, healthcare flexible spending accounts, health care flex plans, POP plans and more. The common characteristics are that the employer offers the employees a choice (cafeteria plan) of fringe benefits, each with its own allowed benefits and dollar limits. The employee may then receive cash wages, or reduce their wages by the amount paid by the employer for the cafeteria benefit chosen by the employee.

The advantage to the employee is that any amounts they tell the employer to spend on their behalf through a cafeteria plan is pre-tax, including Social Security and income tax. Here is a simple example.

Let's say that Dan is a diesel mechanic for a trucking company. Dan's gross pay is $52,500 annually, and Dan's family spends about $2,500 every year on medical bills. Without using a cafeteria plan Dan will pay 7.65% Social Security and an estimated 30% Federal and state income tax on the $52,500, leaving Dan with $36,750 to pay the doctor bills. After paying the doctor bills, Dan is left with $34,250 to live on.

If Dan utilizes his employer's health flex spending account cafeteria plan, Dan tells his employer to reduce his salary by $2,500 and paying up to $2,500 in medical costs on Dan's behalf to the providers. Dan only pays tax on $50,000 (52,500-2,500) which leaves him with $35,000, for $750 more in Dan's pocket by using the flex plan. Or as I like to say, would you rather pay the IRS first (without using a cafeteria plan), or the doctor first, as illustrated below.

<u>No FSA-</u> <u>Pay IRS then Doc</u>		<u>With $2500 FSA-</u> <u>Pay Doc then IRS</u>	
1. Gross Income	$52,500	Gross Income	$52,500
2. Less 30% tax	<u>-15,750</u>	Less FSA Dr.	<u>-2,500</u>
3. Cash left	$ 36,750	Taxable Inc.	$50,000
4. Less Doctor	<u>-2,500</u>	Less 30% Tax	<u>-15,000</u>
5. Cash Left	<u>$ 34,250</u>	Cash Left	<u>$35,000</u>
		Savings $750 in employees hands	

The only disadvantage to the employee of a cafeteria plan is that the amount set aside as a reduction is permanent, meaning if the employee does not use whatever amount is set aside they will not get it back. This is called the use it or lose it rule.

Over 90% of Fortune 500 employers offer cafeteria plans, and an estimated 50% of small employers also offer the plans. The common benefit options in a cafeteria plan may include medical costs (the most common), child care, life insurance, health savings account contributions, disability insurance, and elective vacation days.

Because so many employers offer these fringe benefits everyone must carefully examine their own employee handbook to see what is available. If your employer offers a plan, determine which benefits would be best to you, and then participate fully! The cafeteria plan, because it is misunderstood by many employees, is the second most useful tax shelter available to the average American, with the least participation.

Other Tax Planning Tools

At this point, there is not much left for the average person. If you believe home mortgage interest deductions are good thing you are sadly mistaken. If you pay $10,000 annually in mortgage interest, it will save you, at best, $3,500 so you will still be out of pocket $6,500. Remember we do not have a 100% tax rate in America, and folks that have borrowed against their home "to get the tax deduction" sadly are in early stages of income tax blindness.

If you do have a home mortgage, it would be useful to understand that home mortgage interest, as well as charity and taxes are added together on Schedule A, the itemized deduction form, to see if you can get more deductions by listing (or itemizing) them than you can get by using a given, standard amount. If you can come up with more than the standard amount, consider the simple strategy of bunching. Bunching means to try to get all of your charity deductions in one year, paying as much as you can in January this year, and then again in December of the same year rather than next January. Bunching also applies to medical deductions, although these deductions are very rare nowadays because of tax rules. Work uniforms, dues and the like are very rarely deductible even though everyone tells you to deduct them. In real life, it is unusual to have spent enough on tools, dues and work uniforms to get a deduction.

One other tax planning idea ties back to our discussion of where to invest money from Chapter 3. An individual that invests in real estate is quite often able to legally avoid paying tax on the cash income of rental property using a special deduction called depreciation. If you have rental property, please pay a tax professional to prepare your return because they will get you every deduction available.

Finally, we should address the use of a tax professional. If all you have is a W-2, then do your own return on Turbo Tax. A tax professional should be able to offer you two things: peace of mind and tax savings/planning. A trained professional comes in two forms: licensed and unlicensed. A licensed tax professional is required to take 15-40 hours of income tax related continuing education every year. This group would include an IRS Enrolled Agent (EA) or a California/Oregon/New York licensed tax professional. Members of many national tax associations also require annual tax specific continuing education. In contrast to what the public believes, Certified Public Accountants (CPA) do not have to have *income tax specific* continuing education, their requirement is just for continuing education. The best way to protect yourself is to ask your tax advisor about their annual education. If they receive their education from the IRS they are receiving no education regarding tax planning, just the cheapest update they can get regarding tax rules from people who do not prepare tax returns or provide planning ideas. We advise the general public to carefully check licenses and the source of continuing education classes (non-IRS training) to ensure competent tax advice from planning-trained professionals.

We do not recommend, in most cases, having returns prepared by franchises, unless your individual franchise preparer is an EA, CPA or state licensed individual because we find the knowledge of these people often inadequate. We also never recommend having your return prepared by an unlicensed individual. As founder and President of TaxSpeaker, a national continuing education company for tax professionals teaching continuing education to over 10,000 professionals annually, we see a lot of things out there and we are strong proponents of national licensing, which is sadly lacking other than in the 3-4 states listed and for the EA/CPA. Regular attendees at our classes are tax professionals that I would recommend, because I know what information they are receiving, and yes, I am biased!

6
SO, YOU WANT TO RETIRE?

The earlier you can start saving for retirement, the better, and any amount will do to begin. Thirty years ago, I was a full-time Professor of Accounting for one year at West Virginia Institute of Technology. I deferred about $13,500 into their 401K equivalent plan, and today it has a value of almost exactly $100,000. I have never put another dime in that account. That simple example speaks for itself.

Retirement planners tell us that for most Americans to retire they need about $1 million dollars at retirement. I don't know if that is enough money or not, but I believe it is more than enough for most Americans, and way more than enough if the individuals have followed my "Paid For" rules for having no debt at retirement age. It may not be enough however, for Americans living in big coastal cities.

I think a better way to plan for retirement is to look at how much money you would need to live on annually at retirement age, and compare it to how long you can expect to live. Earlier in the book we saw that the average life expectancy for most Americans is around 85 years old at retirement so we will plan on making sure we have enough money to last 20 years after retirement. We also need to determine an average rate of return on our money and an average inflation rate. Let's be conservative and assume an average annual rate of return of 6%, and an average inflation rate of 3%, for a net annual rate of return on investments after inflation of 3%. Using a 20-year life expectancy, earning a net amount of 3% annually, here is a simple table showing how much you need at retirement to provide for that income.

Annual income desired for 20 years at retirement in today's dollars	Savings amount required at age 65 to provide that annual income
$40,000	$582,461
$50,000	$726,077
$60,000	$873,692
$70,000	$1,019,307
$80,000	$1,164,923

As you can imagine, the variables are unlimited depending on how much you need, actual rates of return, actual inflation rates, actual life, income tax, etc. All we are looking for here are some goals at retirement.

Greg and Teresa will have their home, cars and all debt paid for at age 65. They live in a Midwestern city with low costs and taxes and think that $60,000 in today's dollars annually will provide them with enough income until death. They are both 50 today, and want to know how much they need to put in savings every year, earning 6% annually before 3% inflation to accumulate the roughly $875,000 in today's dollars they will need at age 65. Here is another simple, yet useful table.

Age when savings starts	Annual amount of deposit needed to accumulate $875,000 at age 65
30	$14,472
40	$23,999
45	$32,564
50	$47,046
55	$76,327
60	Never Mind!

How do you determine what you will need at retirement? Hey, here's a wild idea-what about a budget? Remember there will be no mortgage, and clothing and commuting costs will be lower, but medical costs will slowly increase every year and travel costs will probably be high for a few years. I cannot help you here: do your own budget.

What if Greg & Teresa determine that they will be able to get by during retirement with only $40,000 annually in today's dollars, needing only $582,461 at age 65? Let's round that to $600,000 and see what it gets us.

Age when savings starts	Annual amount of deposit needed to accumulate $600,000 at age 65
30	$9,924
40	$16,457
45	$22,329
50	$32,260
55	$52,338
60	$113,013

Our examples are building in inflation and earnings rates at conservative amounts, and for ease of budgeting do everything in today's dollars. And there is one bad flaw in these examples: the money is all gone in twenty years because Greg and Teresa are using both the savings and the earnings during the twenty-year period. Not much else can be said here except start saving, and the sooner the better. Read the previous tax planning chapter for motivation.

Now for the good news. Stealing some information from the Social Security chapter that follows, let's say Greg has earned an average of $60,000 (inflation adjusted) annually every year of his working career. This would provide Greg with a monthly Social Security benefit of about $2,000 starting at age 66, and this amount would continue until his death. His wife Teresa would receive the greater of her own benefit or ½ of Greg's and for conservative purposes let's assume she gets $1,000 monthly in today's dollars. So, while they are both living during retirement Greg and Teresa will receive $3,000 monthly, or $36,000 every year. When one of them does pass away, the monthly family benefit will drop to $2,000 or $24,000 annually.

Here is some interesting information about that Social Security benefit. Although Social Security was never designed as a primary source of retirement income, it does provide a substantial monthly income for average Americans at retirement, and provides a nice savings amount towards the retirement fund that we need to accumulate. A payment of $24,000 annually is the equivalent of a savings account balance at retirement of around $650,000, and the better news is that the payment won't stop if you exceed your life expectancy. If Greg and Teresa each live for 20 years they receive the annual amount of $36,000, which is the equivalent of about $980,000.

Using an equivalent savings account already built in of the $650,000 Social Security monthly annuity check, let's revisit Greg and Teresa's retirement plan. They originally said they needed $60,000 every year in today's dollars to live. It seems that, worst case, Social Security will provide $24,000 annually, so they need to save enough to provide the difference of $36,000 annually. Their savings account at age 65 will need to be $524,215 to provide $36,000 annually if we use the same rates of return and inflation from our previous example.

Age when savings starts	**Annual amount of deposit needed to accumulate $525,000 at age 65**
30	$8,683
35	$11,035
40	$14,400
45	$19,538
50	$28,227
55	$45,796

The charts illustrate exactly what I wanted to illustrate, which is whether you are age 30 or age 55, with adequate planning and a *"Paid For"* approach an adequate retirement income is attainable with some sacrifice.

7
SOCIAL SECURITY TOOLS

The Social Security Administration (SSA) announced in January 2017 that a woman turning 65 in 2017 had an average life expectancy of about 86 ½ years and a man of 84 years. At a time when SSA tells us that about 50% of all Americans are signing up for Social Security as soon as they are eligible at age 62, a lot of these folks are making horrible mistakes. This short chapter is an excerpt from my Amazon book *"2017 Social Security Guide"* at https://www.amazon.com/2017-Social-Security-Guide-Jennings/dp/1542700930 .

Pew Research tells us that 10,000 Americans will be turning 65 every single day for the next fifteen years as the biggest demographic shift in America in history. Most of those turning 65 do not know where to go for advice and are consequently taking advice from everyone but knowledgeable advisors. For example, if you have heard someone say they were taking their Social Security at 62 because "everyone knows it is bankrupt", you can be assured that they do not know what they are talking about-ask them if they have ever read the Social Security trustee's report. Your author has read the bi-partisan, actuarially and demographically based report every year for several years and refuses to fall into political discussions. Here is our opening statement: ***Social Security is not bankrupt and is not going bankrupt in the foreseeable future***

The number one question in America regarding Social Security is "At what age should I sign up?" Bluntly, no one can answer that question except you. Your answer should be based on your analysis of the three factors that determine when you should draw: genetics; personal health; and financial need. The choice to draw at age 62 or waiting until 70 may be the wisest or worst financial decision you will ever make, *depending on this three-factor test.*

Genetics can be summarized as at what age did your ancestors of your sex die (except accidents)? If you are a man and your dad and grandfather died in their 60's then genetics are not on your side. Genetics are not a true indicator, but they play a major part of your decision.

Personal health could be based on the life expectancies provided above, as adjusted downward for smoking, diabetes, kidney disease and obesity. These factors will generally take off about ten years of an individual's life expectancy.

Financial need is a complex factor. All Americans have something called a Full Retirement Age (FRA), which is the age used to determine their monthly benefit check. For most Americans, today it is between 66 and 67. The author's FRA is 66 and his one year old grandson's is 67, so there is not a lot of variation. All Americans may also draw Social Security as early as age 62, but their monthly benefit will be permanently reduced roughly 6% per year for each year they draw early. Conversely, the benefit will increase each year they wait beyond age 66 by about 8% annually until they reach age 70.

Let's say Bob's benefit at his age 66 FRA is $1,000 monthly. Then if Bob draws early at 62 he will only receive about $750 monthly (A $250 monthly reduction I call the "forever penalty"), and if he waits to draw until age 70 he will receive about $1,320 monthly.

But if Bob is married or has dependents drawing on his account as well they will also be affected by Bob's decision to draw. (Later chapters). If Bob draws at 62 he will receive 48 checks of $750 monthly, which also means he will have drawn $36,000 in checks by the time he is 66, ignoring any cost of living increases.

Is there a break-even point between drawing early and paying the forever penalty, and waiting until full retirement age (or longer)? Yes, if Bob waits until 66 to sign up, his check will be $250 more per month than his age 62 check. Since Bob has received $36,000 in early benefits, if you divide the $36,000 in total early benefits received by the $250 monthly difference between the age 62 and 66 benefits, you get 144 months from Bob's full retirement age of 66 or when Bob is age 78 as the break-even point. So, if Bob draws at 62 and lives beyond age 78 this has probably been an unwise financial decision, but if Bob dies before age 78 he has made an excellent choice (financially!). In either event the break-even point is 6 years sooner than his life expectancy.

Age to Draw	62	66	70
Monthly benefit	$750	$1,000	$1,320
Total drawn by age 66	$36,000	$0	$0
Total drawn by age 70	$72,000	$48,000	$0
Total drawn by age 78	$144,000	$144,000	$126,720
Total drawn by age 84	$198,000	$216,000	$221,760

However, we once again ignored annual cost of living increases, which would have a greater positive impact on the larger age 66 benefit than it would on the age 62 benefit. And what about if Bob waited until age 70 to draw, what would be that break-even point? (1320-750=570 more per month at age 70, but Bob would have received 96 checks of 750 or $72,000, divided by 570= 126 months beyond age 70), for a roughly 80 ½ year old break-even point, which is still less than his statistical life expectancy. Are you getting an idea that this stuff is complicated? It would appear based on these simple factors that waiting until age 70 is usually a better choice, but we have ignored cost of living increases, earnings on invested benefits, spousal benefits, dependent benefits, filing strategies and more, all of which will be explained as we go forward. As you are beginning to understand, the decision when to draw is the single most important decision many Americans will ever make, and they are making it without guidance!

Here are a couple of other things that we know. ***Your monthly retirement check at your full retirement age is based on your highest 35 years of earnings from wages and self-employment.*** All those self-employed folks who avoid paying into Social Security with tax write-offs are cutting their own throat at retirement time if they continue this practice after age 30! These are the same folks who are saying it will never be there for me! Guess what, if you don't pay in to the system it won't! And as a 40-year experienced CPA dealing with tens of thousands of clients over the years, we have found that these folks will never invest the difference in Social Security tax savings, and more importantly don't even realize the benefits they are throwing away. Add in the fallacy that they will work until death (statistically never happens!) and these folks are sentenced to an old age of destitution.

If 35 years determines our benefit, then we all have 8-10 years where income doesn't matter, but everything after that does, and taking time off for advanced college, early retirement, child-rearing, etc. has a direct negative impact on retirement.

Finally, SSA tells us this year that the average monthly benefit check for a single American is $1,360. Is that enough for you to live on during retirement? No, and it was never meant to be-Social Security was designed by President Roosevelt to keep Americans from starving to death, not to provide a full retirement check-for that you are on your own. By the way 35 years of paying Social Security tax on $25,000 (inflation adjusted) is what it took to get this $1,360 monthly benefit.

In nearly forty years of practice as a CPA, former CFP® and IRS Enrolled Agent I have discussed income tax, social security, and retirement with literally tens of thousands of clients. When addressing social security issues with clients, particularly those under forty, I am often told, "There will never be anything there for me." This statement has always bothered me because it illustrates a basic lack of understanding by the American consumer (and often their financial adviser) about the benefits provided by the Social Security System.

Let's start with an overview. During 2017 if Average Joe earned $5,200 or more he received the maximum four credits in the Social Security system for the year 2017. This cost him $397.80 if he was a W-2 employee (his employer matched his share) or $795.60 if he was self-employed. If Joe repeats this for nine more years during his life, he has earned complete, minimum coverage under the system. In other words, for a minimum of $3,980 (ten years at $398 per year) Average Joe has received total retirement and medical coverage under the Social Security system.

But what does Joe really get for this $3,980? Our system provides the following benefits to this average Joe for his ten years (forty quarters) of minimum entry-level coverage:

1. A retirement income for Joe starting as early as age sixty-two;
2. A retirement income for Joe's wife, as early as age sixty-two, even if she has never had earned income (age 60 if Joe is dead);
3. A full Medical system at age sixty-five (Medicare) for the remainder of his life;
4. A full Medical system for his wife at age sixty-five, even if she has never had earned income;
5. Disability benefits for Joe in the event of injury today;
6. Disability benefits as early as age fifty for Joe's widow even if she was never covered;
7. Dependent benefits for his disabled, minor, or dependent children, even after Joe's death;

8. Dependent benefits for his dependent parents;
9. Dependent benefit for Joe's wife to care for any children at home under age dependent in the event of Joe's death, disability, or drawing of his retirement benefit;
10. Death benefit for Joe's widow.

Joe gets all of this for $3,980? Yes—possibly the greatest financial investment available to every American, the Social Security system has been misunderstood, maligned, and ignored by nearly everyone. Clearly the system is not meant to be just a retirement plan, it is more precisely a safety net for all Americans, providing rudimentary retirement, disability, and medical coverage at all ages to nearly all Americans. Benefits are not based on need but rather on your payments into the system. The benefits are skewed to provide greater benefits as a percentage of taxed income to lower income earners than to higher income earners.

The Main Categories of Social Security and Medicare Benefits

Retirement benefits can be obtained by workers as early as age sixty-two or delayed until as late as age seventy. The earlier the benefits are first taken, the smaller the benefit and of course, the later the age the benefits are first taken, the larger the benefit. All Americans have an age defined as their full retirement age, usually sixty-five, sixty-six, or sixty-seven, which is dependent on the individual's date of birth. A widow or widower of a covered worker may begin receiving reduced benefits as early as age sixty. To obtain minimal benefits, the retiree must have forty quarters of coverage during his or her lifetime. An individual may qualify for more than one type of benefit such as survivor's benefits as a spouse, as well as his or her own retirement benefit, but may only draw the highest benefit rather than multiple benefits. ***Anyone receiving benefits before their full retirement age will have an actuarial reduction in benefits. This applies to the taxpayer and any spouse or dependents who qualify on the taxpayer's account and who draw benefits prior to their own personal FRA.***

Neither immigrants nor anyone else can collect Social Security benefits without someone paying Social Security payroll taxes into the system. However Social Security is often confused with the Supplemental Security Income (SSI) program. SSI is a federal welfare program and no contributions, from immigrants or citizens or anyone else, is required for eligibility. Under certain conditions, immigrants can qualify for SSI benefits. The SSI program was an initiative of the Nixon Administration and was signed into law by President Nixon on October 30, 1972.

Disability benefits are provided to workers under age sixty-five who have met minimal earned-income requirements. The benefits are like the retirement benefits the employee would receive.

Dependent's benefits are provided to dependent or disabled children and/or parents of the deceased, retired, or disabled Social Security qualified worker based upon the deceased's work history.

Survivor's benefits are provided to the surviving spouse and dependents of a retired or disabled Social Security qualified worker based on the deceased's work history.

Supplemental Security Income (SSI) provides cash assistance to individuals who:

- Have limited income and resources,
- Are age sixty-five or older, or
- Are blind or disabled.

Medicare benefits are various forms of medical coverage provided to retiree's age sixty-five or over, disabled workers, and spouses. Medicare is funded from five sources: payroll tax; interest on old savings accounts; premiums paid by Medicare users; taxes paid by high income beneficiaries; and the General Fund of the United States. The general fund paid over $638 billion in Medicare benefits in 2015 according to the Trustee's report. The Medicare payroll rate is 1.45 percent for both the employee and the employer, and 2.9 percent for the self-employed. There are four types of Medicare benefits.

Medicare hospital insurance (Part A) helps pay for inpatient hospital care, inpatient care in a skilled nursing facility, home health care, and hospice care.

Medicare medical insurance (Part B) helps pay for physician services, outpatient hospital services, outpatient physical therapy, other medical services, and supplies and equipment that are not covered by Part A. The premiums are deducted from Social Security benefits or billed directly to the beneficiary if benefits are not adequate or the retiree is not yet drawing Social Security.

Medicare Advantage Plans (Part C) are plans offered by private companies that contract with Medicare to provide all Medicare Part A and B benefits. They are HMOs, PPOs, or private fee for service plans and some also offer prescription drug coverage. The premiums may, by election, be withheld from the monthly Social Security benefit.

Medicare Prescription Drug Benefit (Part D) provides outpatient prescription drug coverage for the aged and disabled. The premiums may, by election, be withheld from the monthly Social Security benefit.

Summary of Social Security Benefits

Retirees on Their Own Account
40 quarters of employment: benefits may start at age 62 or over.
Spouses Drawing on Worker's Account
Worker had forty quarters of lifetime-covered employment: your benefits may start at 62 or over, but the worker must have started drawing benefits. Your benefit is 50% of the worker's FRA benefit and will be reduced if you are less than your own FRA.
Worker had forty quarters of lifetime-covered employment, and you have a child under age sixteen in your care.
Widows & Widowers Drawing on Deceased Worker's Account
Age sixty and deceased worker had 40 quarters of employment: your benefit is the worker's actual benefit amount, reduced if you begin before your own FRA.
Age fifty and disabled, and deceased worker had forty quarters of employment.
Any age with child under sixteen in your care and your deceased spouse had forty quarters of lifetime-covered employment.
Ex-Spouses Drawing on Ex-Spouse's Account
Married ten or more years, ex-spouse had 40 quarters of lifetime-covered employment: your benefits may start at age 62 if the ex-spouse is still living and at least 62, and you are not currently remarried. Your benefit is 50% of the worker's FRA benefit and will be reduced if you are less than your own FRA.
Married ten or more years, you are age 60 or over, your deceased ex-spouse had forty quarters of lifetime-covered employment, and you are not currently remarried.
Married ten or more years, you are age 50 and disabled, your living/deceased ex-spouse had forty quarters of lifetime-covered employment, and you are not currently remarried.
You are any age, you have a child under age sixteen in your care, your deceased ex-spouse had forty or more quarters of lifetime-covered employment, and you are not currently remarried.

Children
Parent is drawing retirement or disability benefits, and child is under eighteen or under nineteen and still in high school.
Survivor of parent with forty quarters of lifetime-covered employment and under eighteen or under age nineteen if still in high school.
Survivor of parent with forty quarters of lifetime-covered employment, and you are totally disabled before age twenty-two.
Disabled
Forty quarters of lifetime-covered employment and twenty of the last forty quarters of covered employment: benefits may start at any age.
Survivor of parent with forty quarters of lifetime-covered employment and you are totally disabled before age twenty-two.

8
LONG TERM CARE, KIDS AND GRANDKIDS

Long-Term Care Insurance

What is your most valuable asset? Is it your home? What about your car? According to a study from the National Academy of Elder Law Attorneys (www.naela.org) your risk of a house fire is about 1 in 1,200. Your risk of a car wreck is about 1 in 240. You would not think about going without home or car insurance would you? Yet, the most valuable asset you have is yourself and you have about a 1 in 5 chance of requiring long term care assistance according to the United Seniors Health Cooperative and few Americans have long term care insurance. The US Department of Health and Human Services (www.longtermcare.gov) estimates that 70% of Americans over age 65 will need at least some long-term care during the remainder of their life. Women need care longer (3.7 years) then men (2.2 years).

One year of care in a nursing home, based on the 2016 national average, costs over $82,000 for a semi-private room according to www.genworth.com . Many people mistakenly believe that Medicare will pay the cost of nursing care. They are sadly mistaken, as shown in this chart.

Long-Term Care Service	Medicare	Private Medlgap Insurance	Medicaid	Self-Pay
Nursing Home	First 20 days Medicare pays 100% of costs. For days 21-100, you pay $164.50 per day (as of 2017), and Medicare pays balance. You pay 100 % of costs for each day you stay in a skilled nursing facility after day 100.	May pay the co-payment if your nursing home stay meets all other Medicare requirements	May pay for care in a Medicaid certified nursing home if you meet functional and financial eligibility requirements	If you need only personal or supervisory care in a nursing home and/or have not had a prior hospital stay, or if you choose a nursing home that does not participate in Medicaid or is not Medicare certified
Assisted Living & similar facility options	Does not pay	Does not pay	In some states may pay care-related costs but not room and board	Pay on your own except as noted under Medicaid
Continuing care retirement community	Does not pay	Does not pay	Does not pay	Pay on your own
Adult day services	Not covered	Not covered	Varies by state, functional and financial eligibility required	Pay on your own except as noted under Medicaid
Home health care	Limited to reasonable necessary part time/ intermittent skilled nursing care or home health aide services, and some doctor-ordered therapies provided by a Medicare certified home health agency.	Not covered	Will pay, but some states have option to limit some services, such as therapy	Pay on your own except as noted under Medicaid

What is long-term care?

Long-term care includes a variety of services and supports to meet health or personal care needs over an extended period of time. Most long-term care is non-skilled personal care assistance, such as help performing the six everyday Activities of Daily Living (ADLs), which are:

1. Bathing,
2. Dressing,
3. Using the toilet,
4. Transferring (to or from bed or chair),
5. Caring for incontinence, and
6. Eating.

The US Government estimates that the average length of long term care is for three years, with about 20 percent of Americans over 65 needing care for more than five years.

Long-term care is expensive. Costs for long-term care services vary greatly depending on the type and amount of care you need, the provider you use, and where you live. For example, many care facilities charge extra for services provided beyond the basic room-and-board charge, although some may have "all inclusive" fees. Home health and home care services are usually provided in two-to-four-hour blocks of time referred to as "visits." An evening, weekend or holiday visit may cost more than a weekday visit. Some community programs, such as adult day service programs, are provided at a per-day rate, and rates may differ based on the type and variety of programs and services offered.

It's difficult to predict if or how much care you will need, whether you will have family or friends who can provide some or all your care, and how much care may cost you. However, it's reasonably easy to predict that if you need extensive long-term care services or need services over a long period, you will have to pay for some or all of it out of your personal finances. That's why an increasing number of people are using private financing options to help them pay for long-term care if and when they need it.

Private long-term care financing options include long-term care insurance, trusts, annuities, and reverse mortgages. Which option is best for you depends on many factors including your age, your health status, your risk of needing long-term care, and your personal financial situation. We will only discuss long term care insurance in this manual.

The 5 Requirements for good long-term care policies:

1. An elimination (waiting) period of 180 days or less;
2. Minimum coverage of $200 per day;
3. An inflation protection clause;
4. Home care coverage;
5. The benefit period should provide a minimum of 3 years of protection.

What is Long-Term Care Insurance?

Long-term care insurance is a type of insurance developed specifically to cover the costs of long-term care services, most of which are not covered by traditional health insurance or Medicare. These include services in your home such as assistance with Activities of Daily Living as well as care in a variety of facility and community settings.

There is a great deal of choice and flexibility in long-term care insurance policies. You can select a range of care options and benefits that allow you to get the services you need in the settings that suit you best. The cost of your long-term care insurance policy is based on the type and amount of services you choose to have covered, how old you are when you buy the policy, and any optional benefits you choose, such as Inflation Protection. If you are in poor health or already receiving long-term care services, you may not qualify for long-term care insurance, or you may only be able to buy a more limited amount of coverage, or buy coverage at a higher "non-standard" rate.

Long-term care insurance policies have a benefit period or lifetime benefit maximum, which is the total amount of time or total number of dollars up to which benefits will be paid. Common benefit periods for long-term care policies are two, three, four, and five years, and lifetime or unlimited coverage. Other options between five years and lifetime/unlimited coverage are also available from many companies. Most policies translate these time periods into dollar amounts and do not actually limit the number of days for which they will pay for care – just the overall dollar amount that the policy will pay. There are fewer companies today willing to offer an unlimited/lifetime policy, although some have a "high coverage option" like a $1 million lifetime limit.

With long-term care insurance, you pay premiums in amounts you know in advance and can budget for, and the policy pays – up to its coverage limits – for the long-term care you need when you need it. Typically, premiums are waived during the time you are receiving benefits.

Paid for

Policy and Benefit Choices

The following is a summary of policy and benefit choices:

- You select a daily benefit amount (for example, $100/day), which is the maximum daily amount of expenses for care the policy will pay. Most policies let you choose from $50/day to as much as $500/day. A growing number of policies specify benefits in terms of a monthly amount so that you have the flexibility to receive more care on some days (for example, when family care is not available) and less care on other days.

- Often you can choose whether you want the policy to pay the same daily benefit amount for care in all settings, or whether you want the policy to pay less for care in less costly settings, such as home care. Common choices include a home care benefit of 50 percent or 75 percent of the daily nursing home benefit amount.

- You choose a Maximum Lifetime Benefit or total lifetime amount you want the policy to provide. Policies typically offer a choice of lifetime dollar amounts – for example $100,000 or $300,000. The dollar amounts may correspond to a period of time. For example, a three-year policy at $100/day of benefits would provide you with a total of $109,500 for care. Some insurers also sell "Lifetime" or "Unlimited" coverage that has no dollar limit; you receive benefits as long as you continue to need long-term care and receive covered services.

- You choose the type of coverage you prefer – "comprehensive" or "facility care only." Comprehensive policies cover a wider range of care settings and services including both care at home and in various types of facilities.

- Most policies today are comprehensive, but some people prefer to buy facility care only policies. These pay for care in a nursing home or assisted living facility, but not for care at home or in the community. These policies may still include hospice or respite care but only when those services are provided in a facility. Facility-care-only policies cost less than comprehensive policies, and if people prefer and have family or friends to provide care at home, they may only have the policy to reimburse them for paid care in a facility if and when they need it.

- Many policies offer additional optional "riders" allowing you to customize coverage. One important option is Inflation Protection, which helps protect you from the rising cost of care over time. Most people who buy long-term care insurance opt for an inflation protection rider which builds the cost in to the starting premium, so the cost of the policy doesn't increase simply because the value of the coverage increases with inflation. But there are many different types of Inflation Protection in long-term care insurance.

- Most policies offer benefits in a variety of settings, such as your home, an adult day care center, an assisted living community, or a nursing home.

Additional Costs Long-Term Care Insurance Sometimes Covers

Many policies may also pay for services or devices to support people living at home:

- Equipment such as in-home electronic monitoring systems.

- Home modification, such as grab bars and ramps,

- Transportation to medical appointments,

- Training for a friend or relative to learn to provide personal care safely and appropriately

Some policies provide some payment for family members or friends to help care for you, but may do so on a limited basis, or only in relation to the costs that the family member incurs. The 2010 average reported national cost of a home health aide was about $22 per hour.

Many policies provide the services of a care coordinator, usually a nurse or social worker in your community. The care coordinator can meet with you and discuss your specific personal situation, and help arrange for and monitor your care. The care coordinator's help is usually optional – you use it if you need and want it – and you are not limited to the providers that the care coordinator may recommend.

What Is a Typical Comprehensive Long-Term Care Insurance Benefit?

The majority of policies sold today are comprehensive policies. They typically cover care and services in a variety of long-term care settings:

- Your home, including skilled nursing care, occupational, speech, physical and rehabilitation therapy, as well as help with personal care, such as bathing and dressing. Many policies also cover some homemaker services, such as meal preparation or housekeeping, in conjunction with the personal care services you receive;
- Adult day health care centers;
- Hospice care;
- Respite care;
- Assisted living facilities (also called residential care facilities or alternate care facilities);
- Alzheimer's special care facilities; and
- Nursing homes

What Does Long-Term Care Insurance Cost?

Policy costs vary greatly based on your age at the time of purchase, the policy, and the coverage you select. We are fans of policies purchased in your late 40's because Alzheimer's tests are usually required beginning at age 50.

The American Association for Long Term Care Insurance reports the following average 2016 annual premium prices for a comprehensive long-term care policy with a 90-day waiting period, inflation protection, 100% home care benefit and skilled care coverage for 3 years at $150 maximum daily benefit.

Age 55 single:	$1,800 annually
Age 55 couple (shared policy):	$3,266 annually
Age 60 Couple (shared policy)	$3,881 annually

How Do You Pay Long-Term Care Insurance Premiums?

Different policies offer different payment options. With most policies, you pay premiums according to a schedule you select - monthly, quarterly, semi-annually or annually. You may be able to have the premium automatically withdrawn from your bank account, pension check, or paycheck (if you obtain coverage through your employer). Typically you pay premiums until you begin to receive benefits. Then premiums are waived as long as you continue to receive benefits.

With most policies, you pay premiums as long as you are not receiving benefits. However, with some policies you pay premiums only for a specified period – most often 10, 15, or 20 years. For example, with the 20-year option, you pay a monthly premium for 20 years and then your coverage is fully paid up. If you begin to receive benefits before the 20-year pay period is over, you stop paying premiums while you are receiving benefits. If you recover and have not yet paid in for all 20 years, you resume payments. With some policies you only pay premiums until age 65.

A few companies offer a "Single Pay" option, in which you pay for the insurance in one lump sum payment. While they are more expensive than traditional long-term care insurance, the advantage is that the single lump sum payment is the only premium required. These policies typically pay for long-term care expenses and also offer you the option to include a death benefit for your heirs. Some states do not allow single-pay policies.

When Are Long-Term Care Benefits Paid?

When benefits are paid is based on the policy's "benefit trigger," the length of the elimination period you choose, and sometimes when you start receiving paid care.

Policies use objective measures to determine when you need long-term care. These are called 'benefit triggers.' Most policies use Activities of Daily Living and Cognitive Impairment as triggers for benefits. The policy pays benefits when you need help with two or more of the six Activities of Daily Living or when you have a Cognitive Impairment.

Benefits begin to be paid after an elimination period has elapsed. This is the number of days between when a benefit trigger occurs and when you begin to receive payment for services. An elimination period is like the deductible you have on your car insurance, except it is usually specified as a period of time rather than a dollar amount. As noted above, most policies allow you to choose the length of the elimination period, generally 30, 60 or 90 days. During the elimination period, you are responsible for the cost of any services you receive. Policies differ with regard to whether you are required to receive paid care or pay for services to satisfy an elimination period before benefits start.

Once you are eligible for benefits, most policies reimburse the costs you incur for covered services up to a pre-set limit. Some policies simply pay you a pre-set cash amount for each day that you meet the 'benefit trigger' whether you receive paid long-term care services or not. These "cash disability" policies offer greater flexibility but are also significantly more expensive.

Paid for

Consumer Protections

The following rules apply to all long-term care insurance policies:

- Coverage cannot be cancelled or not renewed as long as you continue to pay premiums as they are due and you have not used up the maximum policy benefits.
- You have 30 days after receiving the policy to return it for a full refund.
- You have the right to designate another person to receive notice of premiums due and payments missed so you won't accidentally miss a payment.
- You have up to 65 days after the date a premium payment is due to make payment. Coverage cannot be cancelled for non-payment until after the grace period and until the "third party designee" has also been notified.
- If coverage lapses for non-payment because you were "disabled" at the time, you can restore your coverage within five months of the missed premium due date.
- If you have a group policy through your employer or other association, you can continue that coverage, unchanged, if you leave the group but want to maintain the policy.
- A spouse insured through an employer group plan may maintain coverage even after a divorce.
- Your premiums are designed to remain level over the lifetime of your coverage, and are based on your age when you first buy the policy. The insurer can change rates on a group (or class) basis, but has only a limited right to do so, and the change must apply to an entire group or class. You cannot be singled out for a rate increase.
- In most states, rate increases must be filed with and approved by the State Department of Insurance. Many states have adopted regulations that make it very difficult for an insurer to obtain approval for a rate increase.
- You typically have the right to decrease your coverage, without underwriting, if you find in the future that the current premium costs are beyond your financial means.

Where to Buy Long-Term Care Insurance

Most people buy long-term care insurance directly from an insurance agent, financial planner or broker. States regulate which companies can sell long-term care insurance and the products that they can sell. There are over 100 companies offering long-term care insurance nationally, however about 15 to 20 insurers sell most of the policies on the market today. The best way to find out which insurance companies offer this type of coverage in your state is to contact your state's Department of Insurance:

http://www.consumeraction.gov/insurance.shtml

Another option for some people is to buy long-term care insurance offered through their employer. Many private and public employers, including the Federal government and a growing number of state governments, offer group long-term care programs as a voluntary benefit. Employers do not typically contribute to the premium cost (as they do with health insurance), but they often negotiate a favorable group rate.

Partnership Policies

A Partnership Program is a collaboration or "partnership" among a state government, the private insurance companies selling long-term care insurance in that state, and state residents who buy long-term care Partnership policies. The purpose of the Partnership program is to make the purchase of shorter term more comprehensive long-term care insurance meaningful by linking these special policies (called Partnership qualified or PQ policies) with Medicaid for those who continue to require care.

Partnership qualified policies must meet special requirements that can differ somewhat from state to state. Most states require Partnership policies to offer comprehensive benefits (cover institutional and home services), be Tax Qualified, provide certain specific consumer protections, and include state specific provisions for inflation protection. Often the only difference between a partnership qualified policy and other long-term care insurance policies sold in a state is the amount and type of inflation protection required by the state.

Partnership policies must be certified by the State as meeting the specific requirements for the Partnership Program.

Deferred Annuities with Long Term Care Insurance

Usually best for individuals at or above retirement age, annuities are now offered by many insurers, including Genworth Financial, Prudential and Transamerica. The advantage of this form of annuity is the guaranteed return or value for the buyer and their heirs. The disadvantages include lack of inflation protection and a reduced rate of return over conventional annuities. Tax rules now allow tax-free distributions from the annuity to pay for long term care.

Under this type of plan payments are made over a long period of time for the annuity's life with accumulating earnings on a tax-free basis. The policy then allows normal annuity features such as fixed payment amounts and dates. Where the policy differs is a long-term care rider that specifies when the long-term care provision kicks in, how long and how much it will pay, and how it affects the existing annuity payments. The long-term care provision should be similar to a normal good long term care policy.

Life Insurance with Long Term Care Insurance

Several insurers are offering this alternative to long term care policies, including John Hancock, Lincoln Financial, Nationwide, Genworth Life and OneAmerica. The advantage of this policy is evident, with guaranteed life insurance protection combined with a long-term care rider. An unusual advantage of this type of policy is that it usually offers a full premium refund at any time without penalty, and there is no risk that long-term care coverage costs will increase. The negative with these types of policies is that they reduce the life insurance protection provided as the long-term care provision is used.

Can Everyone Buy Long-Term Care Insurance?

No, having certain conditions means you may not qualify for long-term care insurance. However, insurance companies have different standards, so while you may be denied coverage by one company, another might accept you. You will probably not be approved to purchase a policy if:

- You currently use long-term care services.
- You already need help with Activities of Daily Living.
- You have AIDS or AIDS Related Complex (ARC).
- You have Alzheimer's disease or any form of dementia or cognitive dysfunction.
- You have a progressive neurological condition such as Multiple Sclerosis or Parkinson's Disease.
- You have had a stroke within the past 12 to 24 months or a history of strokes or multiple Transient Ischemic Attacks (TIAs).
- You have metastatic cancer (cancer that has spread beyond its original site).

Other health conditions are evaluated in deciding whether or not you can obtain the insurance, but these are the primary conditions that can disqualify you from obtaining insurance.

Once you are accepted for coverage, your coverage cannot be cancelled for any reason other than non-payment of premium as due, or if you have received the policy's maximum benefits. If you develop one of the health conditions listed above after obtaining coverage, you would be covered for the care you need for that condition.

Long Term Care Insurance Summary

Long term care insurance is an expensive policy to purchase. It is not for everyone because of its cost, particularly when Medicaid will pay for long term care. What you need to realize is that Medicaid varies state-by-state, and most states require that nearly all of your money be used up before it will pay anything, and then in most states Medicaid only pays for a shared room in Spartan conditions with care provided only at the minimum standards required by law. My wife and I both have it because our parents all ended up needing long term care, we did not want to burden our kids with any issues, and we were (and are) willing to sacrifice to buy the policies.

Saving for Kids

Don't open that plain old savings account for a newborn or small child-there are better options. There is a special account that Congress set up for the average American child called a Coverdell Education Savings Account, or ESA, that is perfect for the average kid. This is a special account that allows up to $2,000 of contributions for the child in a year from anyone, not just the parent. This limit is per child, not per person setting up the account. The amount that goes into the account is not tax deductible, but none of the earnings on the account are taxable, they can be withdrawn tax-free for school related costs until the child reaches age 30, and can even be used for computers, parochial school, kindergarten, and just about anything school-related other than home schooling.

Parents often hear about these things called 529 accounts, which allow you to put two hundred thousand or more dollars into a college fund. That really sounds great, but in real life most folks are lucky to come up with a few hundred dollars each year, much less a few hundred thousand, so always fund the ESA. If you have more money than that for your child, great, then look at the other investment ideas discussed in chapter three, or read on to the 529 plan discussion that follows, but here is your number one rule for kid's savings accounts: open an ESA. To get one, go to www.TDAmeritrade.com and open one with a few hundred dollars out of the child's savings account. Yes, the child may have both an ESA and a 529 plan. It doesn't take $2,000 to start an account, you can start it with as little as $100, but the maximum deposit per year is $2,000 from all sources.

Once an ESA is funded, it is also a good life-learning tool to have the child setup a savings account on their own. I strongly believe that the child should be told about their "college account" early on, as a college motivator for the child, and as a reminder to the parent that the money is for education, not consumption. The non-ESA savings account should be setup for the child to make regular deposits, and establish a goal with your child early on that "once the account hits xx dollars, we will buy you a laptop". The goal should be 10% or more higher than the expected cost of the item so that the account can then continue to be used for another goal.

Some parents establish a Uniform Gift to Minors Account or UGMA for their kids. I am not a fan of these accounts because they offer no special tax treatment and when the child reaches age 18 the child controls the money. With an ESA, the parent controls the money until the child is age 30, and the tax benefits are significant.

The ESA benefit applies to expenses for Kindergarten through college, including private schools. This distinct pre-college use advantage of the ESA means that ESAs should always be established before 529 plans. Earnings on the account are tax-deferred. Withdrawals from the account, if used for education expenses, are tax-free.

Coverdell ESA Q&A	
What is a Coverdell ESA?	A savings account that is set up to pay the qualified education expenses of a designated beneficiary
Where can I open a Coverdell ESA?	At any US bank or IRS approved entity
Who can have a Coverdell ESA?	Any beneficiary under 18 or with special needs
Are contributions deductible?	No
Are earnings taxed while in the ESA?	No
Are withdrawals from the ESA subject to tax?	Only if the withdrawals are more than the beneficiary's qualified education expenses for the year
What is the annual contribution limit per designated beneficiary?	$2,000 per each beneficiary
What if more than one Coverdell ESA has been opened for the same beneficiary?	The annual contribution limit is $2,000 for each beneficiary no matter how many accounts exist for that beneficiary or how many individuals contribute.
Can contributions of stock or bonds be made to a Coverdell ESA?	Only cash contributions are allowed.
When must contributions stop?	No contributions may be made to a beneficiary's account after they reach 18, except for special needs beneficiaries.

Once a child begins earning wages, make sure that they also start putting money into a Roth IRA, and there is no minimum age for a Roth contribution. The maximum contribution in one year is $5,500 if they have that much income, and the money may be withdrawn without penalty after five years for college and as a down payment for a new home under certain guidelines. Yes, I am a fan of this treatment as well.

When my son Ryan came to work for me at age 12, he fully funded the Roth IRA each year, out of his own earnings, up to what he made. *He says he doesn't remember doing this but I swear he said he wanted to save it for his retirement, and I know money went into his Roth in those early years!* Today, as a thirty-year-old married man with kids of his own, the money is still in the account (he did not use it for college or a first home), and he has a great start on retirement with the amount involved. Because of his age at the beginning, we invested it in a Vanguard balanced-goal (return/growth) mutual fund where it still resides today.

For their two children Aria and Kiernan, Ryan and his wife Casey fund their individual ESA's every year to the full $2,000 with gifts from us to do so. This enables their kids to also benefit from the ESA tax advantages, and we started this plan the year each child was born. The older child, Aria, at five years old just hit a $10,000 balance in her Ameritrade account, and we moved the money (while staying with Ameritrade) from the general money market savings account used to accumulate $10,000 to the same mutual fund her father is in. The younger child, Kiernan, only has $4,000 in the account right now, but once the account hits $10,000 we will do the same thing. And once each child is old enough to go to work, they will also put a major portion of their earnings into Roth IRAs. Here is a key factor for a parent with a working child: don't ask, tell. I mean don't ask the child if they want to put money into the account, tell them they will put money into the account.

Saving for Grandkids

After making sure that grandkid's ESAs are fully funded, if a grandparent wants to do more to help the child, set up a 529 plan. The average American does not need some fancy trust or stock holdings, they need every tax and savings advantage available, and the 529 allows the grandparent to set aside more money for the grandkids in a tax advantaged manner than anything else. There is no requirement to fully fund it-any amount will do. Many states offer state tax deductions or credits as well, so investigate this one closely.

Here is what we have done for our own grandkids. My wife and I each put $5,000 annually into the older child's 529 plan. We do this because our home state of Indiana allows a special tax benefit up to $5,000. We then gift our son and his wife the same amount of money and have them then use that money to make a similar 529 plan contribution and obtain the same state tax benefit. Use the oldest child to fully fund the account because any unspent money may always be transferred to the next younger sibling or relative. We set the account trustee as our son rather than us, because he will outlive us, but he will keep the grandkids from frivolously spending the money. Much of understanding a 529 plan requires some tax knowledge, but here is some basic information.

A qualified tuition program (QTP) (also known as a 529 plan or program) is a program set up to allow you to either prepay, or contribute to an account established for paying, a student's qualified education expenses at an eligible educational institution. Whoever purchases the Section 529 plan is the custodian and controls the funds until they are withdrawn. One of our favorite sources for information on 529 plans is www.savingforcollege.com .

QTPs can be established and maintained by states (or agencies or instrumentalities of a state) and eligible educational institutions. Because multiple accounts may be established the taxpayer is not restricted to one specific state operated 529, even if already funded.

There is no deduction at the federal level for contributions to 529 plans, although many states offer a state credit or deduction. Earnings are not subject to federal tax and generally not subject to state tax when used for the qualified education expenses of the designated beneficiary, such as tuition, fees, books, as well as room and board. You can set one up and name anyone as a beneficiary — a relative, a friend, even yourself. There are no income restrictions on either you, as the contributor, or the beneficiary. There is also no limit to the number of plans you set up.

Unlike Custodial Accounts and ESAs, 529 plans allow the account owner to maintain control over the assets in a 529 plan for the life of the account. You also can change beneficiaries to another "family member" of the original beneficiary. Thus, if your child gets a scholarship or decides not to go to college, you can name another beneficiary, even yourself.

Some 529 plans, especially prepaid tuition plans, may limit or restrict your ability to change beneficiaries, so check the plan offering document. The assets of one 529 plan can be transferred tax-free to another 529 plan of another beneficiary, if the new beneficiary is a "family member" of the beneficiary of the 529 plan from which the transfer was made. "Family members" include, among others, the beneficiary's spouse, son, daughter, grandchild, niece, nephew, and first cousin.

There are two types of 529 plans—***prepaid tuition plans*** and ***college savings plans.*** Every state offers at least one of these types of plans. Some states offer both, and now a consortium of private colleges also offers a prepaid tuition plan. Make sure to speak with your tax advisor regarding these plans to make sure you understand the rules, or look for our short book on education savings plans on Amazon, or by calling us at 877-466-1040.

Paid for

Section 529 **Plan Comparisons**

Prepaid Tuition Plans	**College Savings Plans**
Tuition and fees only	Tuition, fees, books & supplies
Room & Board usually not covered	Room & Board if at least ½ time
Lock in current tuition rates	Not directly protected against tuition increases
Must be resident of state offering plan	Not limited to specific school or even state
May have age /grade limits	No age/grade limits
No investment options	Many investment options
Transferability limited for other schools to equivalent tuition	Fully transferable to other schools
May be transferred to siblings	Fully transferrable to other family members
Refund usually limited to deposit	Fully refundable

9
PLANNING FOR BAD THINGS

How NOT to buy a House

In April, 1980 after 18 months of working two and even three jobs apiece, Jean and I had saved enough money to buy our first home. Of the two things we did right buying our first home, the 20% down payment was one of them. We will get to the other right thing, but first let's talk about everything we did wrong buying the house.

We started our house search by hiring a realtor who was a family friend of my in-laws. We told him what we wanted, and what we did not want and he apparently listened to nothing because he showed us three homes that met none of our desires, but were listed by him. That was a good life lesson-never hire a realtor that wants to sell you a home, hire a realtor that wants you to help you buy a home. If a realtor does not listen to your desires and make suggestions for improvements, change realtors. I immediately fired him, thinking we could do better on our own. A friend of ours was selling a nice home in our small river town and offered to finance the home, so we bought the house.

Mistake one was not negotiating on the asking price. Mistake two was buying the nicest home in the neighborhood, and, combining that with mistake one, having too much money invested in the highest priced home in the neighborhood! Our learning points on those first two mistakes were to always negotiate on a price, and never buy the most expensive house in the subdivision if you ever plan on selling it. *Always ask yourself how easy or difficult it will be to resell a house in the future!* It is difficult to sell the nicest home in the subdivision, and it is difficult to sell one or two bedroom homes and one bath homes, just as it is difficult to sell homes at the bottom of a hill (water issues), homes near major highways or railroad lines (noise) or homes near industrial areas. In many areas of the country it is also difficult to sell homes with swimming pools (but not in perennially warm climates).

Mistake three was our failure to get the house inspected. The home had been built cheaply in the 1970's, in an era when many homes were built with aluminum, rather than copper wiring. This is a major fire risk as well as a major pain in the rear when repairing outlets, and a major deterrent upon resale. The home was also built near the Ohio river, an area notorious for termites, and we failed to get a termite inspection. We also failed to get a fireplace inspection and found that neither of the two fireplaces could handle the high temperatures of a wood stove. Yes, this was home buying brilliance indeed. The lesson here is simple. Always have the home inspected for age and problems, as well as code compliance with wiring, plumbing, heating/cooling, sewer, roof, bugs and radon, as well as encroachments, zoning, liens and easements.

Mistake four was one of just plain inexperience. This was a two-story home with one bedroom, bath and living room on the first floor, and one bedroom, bath, den, living room, kitchen and laundry on the second floor. A two-bedroom home is very difficult to resell and not suitable at all for the kids we hoped to have.

Mistake five was much worse however, the mistake we made regarding heating and cooling systems. In a state like Indiana, with four defined seasons of the year, there are wide temperature variations, and a two-story home needs either separate systems to heat and cool each floor, or special vent zoning for each floor. Without it, the location of the thermostat will always make one floor's temperature greatly different than the others. We found the first floor in our home ice cold in winter with the thermostat upstairs (heat rises), and ice cold in the summer because the southern exposure to the second floor next to the thermostat also made the upstairs too hot. When looking at heating/cooling systems generally avoid boiler heat (costly repairs) and non-air conditioned homes in most areas of the country. Even if you think you can avoid the cost of air conditioning, the resale is very difficult. We owned a home once in which we installed a geothermal system which ran flawlessly, but I would get it carefully checked before I bought a home with an existing geothermal or solar system. Obtain copies of 12-36 months of utility bills and ask for repairmen references.

Mistake six was buying the home on contract. We were lucky and had no issues when we did refinance the home several years later, except that one of the two contract owners had died, and we needed to have extra legal work done with his surviving widow! We never realized it, but the deduction for home mortgage interest on a home bought on contract is also in jeopardy if the contract is not recorded at the courthouse.

Mistake seven was not going to a local bank to obtain the mortgage. With a 20% down payment, we would have been able to get conventional financing, it was just easier to buy it "on contract" at a rate of interest that frankly was higher than we could have obtained at the local bank.

Mistake eight was our failure to obtain replacement cost insurance on the home *and contents.* We never needed it, but after my CFP training I learned to always purchase that type of coverage.

Our other "right thing" made up for many of these mistakes however, because we had pride of ownership. The home had been badly neglected for the last year, but had tremendous potential and we proceeded to clean, paint and repair in every spare minute. The very large yard was crammed with fruit trees, berry bushes and a large garden area, but had not been cut or maintained in a couple of years, and I proceeded to work all summer cleaning up the yard, trimming the fruit trees and blackberries and raspberries, planting a huge garden and cleaning up several years' worth of trash. By that fall we had accomplished a lot, the house looked great, the yard was in fine condition and we were eating our own produce and fruit just before the bottom dropped out.

<u>You've got six months to live</u>

After buying our first home at 27 years old for me, 25 for Jean, I continued to work three jobs to accumulate some cash again, and every night and spare moment I cleared brush and worked aggressively in the yard to get it to the standards we wanted. I noticed each night that I was worn out, but just attributed it to 80-hour work weeks and 40-hour home repair weeks. By mid-summer 1980 however I was awakening every morning drenched in sweat, working the horrendous hours through sheer willpower, and I noticed a small growth in my upper thigh. By mid-September the growth was the size of a golf ball, and I finally went to my long-time friend and personal doctor to have him look at the growth. During the brush clearing I had been scratched by a feral cat living in the weeds, and bitten and stung by any insect living within 500 yards and he thought I might have something called cat-scratch fever (yes there is such a thing). In those days there were no "out-patient clinics", so we scheduled a surgical removal the next week at the hospital.

The surgery was performed by our local surgeon, Dr. Gordon, and it wasn't really a major thing. Again, times were different, but I was not able to be discharged until lab results came back a day or two later. When the lab results came in, Gordon called my room and said he would send my personal doctor Freedie to speak with me. Freedie walked in the room an hour or so later with a strange look, and when I asked him what was wrong with him he turned and walked out of the room. I took this as a bad sign.

A little later Freedie came back in and told me I had some type of cancer I had never heard of involving the lymphatic system and that I needed to speak with someone called an oncologist, something I had never heard of either. Two hours later I was introduced to the most brilliant man I have ever known, Dr. Stan. He told me what I had and explained that I needed two or three more major surgeries to determine the extent and the treatment needed. He had absolutely no bedside manner and I immediately loved him because of his frank nature. After the other two surgeries, Stan told me they had removed my spleen and determined that I also had liver involvement in a Stage 4 cancer. (There are 4 stages).

Stan was very upfront and answered all my questions, as well as providing me with the first hints of where we are going with this chapter. He told me to get my life in order now, because without an aggressive treatment that would probably kill me on its own, I had 6 months left to live. He then asked me if I would go through psychological testing to see if I was suited for his aggressive chemotherapy treatment and to this day I am not sure if I passed or failed! I do know the next eight months were horrific, but I lived and continue to live nearly forty years later. Two non-medical things remain with me to this day: first, his directive to get things in order (without any guidance how to do that); and second, for the only time I can ever remember before or since, I felt lost.

Upon returning home from talking with Dr. Stan, I felt sorry for myself for a couple of hours and went for a walk on the river with my dog, lost literally and mentally. I returned home a couple of hours later with a resolve to beat this thing, retain my sense of humor, and figure out what he meant by "getting your life in order", and then do it. Hoping for the best, you plan for the worst and my resolve and decision to plan came that day on the banks of the Ohio River in southern Indiana.

Over the next nearly 40 years I have seen dozens of clients who never got their life in order, and upon a death, stroke or major illness the remaining spouse or family members are also lost, having no idea what to do, where to start, what they have or don't have, and most importantly, where to look for information. That first life event with Dr. Stan, modified and transformed by 40 years of client experience has led to the guidance that follows, something I call "The Death Book", but which we should probably call by a lighter name, so let's call it "The Life Book" because it is written for your survivors.

Think about who handles the financial information in your family. If that person were to suddenly die today of an accident, would you know where to start, what you have, answers to the daily challenges like what bills to pay and how to pay them, or even where the information is kept? Well that is what "The Life Book" is going to do, it is going to lead you out of the lost woods! Keep The Life Book in a fireproof safe at home, with access to the safe available to your significant other, if any, and at least one other trusted person.

Let's begin by obtaining a large 3" three-ring binder. Now, I know many of you are going to say no, I want to keep it on the computer. Great idea-if you are killed in a car wreck coming home from the bookstore after buying this book, what is the password to log on to your computer? And what is the file name of the information? And what is the name of the folder where that file is kept? Your survivors will not know any of these things. Keep the book in physical format in a secure area, and use it to refer to the hard drive if needed.

After you get the binder, buy some tabs to separate the topics in the binder. Label the tabs as follows: banking; financial; retirement; insurance; investments; and other. We will discuss what should be in each tab, but remember what the goal of "The Life Book" should be: it should guide your survivors in what to do in the event of your death or illness. As a side benefit, it will also help you obtain a firm handle on what you have, what you owe, how much insurance you have, and identify shortfalls in your planning.

The first page of the book should be a personal directive letter from you to your survivors, saying whatever you think is important. Keep it positive-do you really want to be remembered as a grudge-holding jerk? I think that some thank you's are appropriate, combined with appreciation and guidance. The guidance should be what to do at your funeral, where and how to be interred, and some general ideas outside of your will of what you would like to see done with any remaining money. This is not a legal document, it is a practical document. The letter should be followed by copies of your wills and medical care directives, and state where the original copies of these items are maintained. This is a very private document, but I have reprinted some pertinent sections of my own to provide you with some general ideas.

Also preceding the first tab should be some copies of important legal documents. I am not an attorney so my advice will be general. If you die without a will in most states your assets will be divided under state law, which will divide things up in a totally different manner than most people wish. Go to an attorney and draw up a simple will. Don't do it online and don't do it yourself-think of the will as an insurance policy that protects your wishes, with a one-time cost of a few hundred dollars per person, so don't cut corners. Newlyweds need wills, even before they have assets; single folks and unmarried live-togethers need wills; everyone needs them. While you have the local attorney draw up the will, also have the attorney draw up a durable power of attorney, which will allow someone you trust to act on your behalf if you are unable to make decisions, and also have the attorney draw up a medical directives agreement explaining what to do in the event of your inability to decide your own fate.

As you go through certain areas accumulating The Life Book, you will find shortcomings in your own planning. Make physical notes of these shortfalls, prioritize them and then set and not goals to fix the shortfalls. Use the checklists provided at the end of the book.

Some very common mistakes that we see are the failure to name (and update) beneficiaries on life insurance policies, and the failure to name and update beneficiaries on retirement accounts. These are critical errors that can be addressed easily in life, but not at all after death.

Reprinted below is an abbreviated version of selected information from my own Life Book to provide you an indication of the information that should be at the beginning of the Life Book.

Microsoft One Drive (Personal) on my home computer has all personal information including financial, tax and insurance stuff. The login to my home computer is xxxxx (Remember the Life Book must be kept in a secure area, and tell your spouse/other/heir where it is. Mine is kept in a locked closet and disguised in such a manner that protects it and its contents, and the login to the computer is one known only to me, my wife and my son and daughter-in-law.)

DropBox has all business information for :xxxx

Checking & Savings access-these are all the accounts we have:

Personal Checking is with xxxx, account xxxx-online login is through Dashlane password protection. Automatic withdrawals are setup for xxxxx, xxxx and xxxx every month in the amounts of xxxx,xxxx,xxxx each.

Check register is maintained electronically in Quicken on Bob's home computer, backups are on OneDrive.

Business Checking is with xxxx, account xxxx-online login is xxxx through Dashlane. Automatic withdrawals are setup for xxxxx.

Check register is in QuickBooks online, login is xxxx through DashLane on home or either office or laptop computer.

Jean owns xxxx stock personally, xxxx stock is owned jointly with xxxx-, there are no other investments except Vanguard account xxxx. Online login to Vanguard is xxxx through Dashlane on home computer or laptop.

OneDrive (Personal) "Financial Statements" Excel file is hyperlinked where possible to many accounts and has current detail.

OneDrive (Personal) file "Life Ins" has current life policy details-see my home desk bottom left drawer for policies.

OneDrive (Personal) Folder has all tax returns (plus in file cabinet in home office closet), extra will copies and other pertinent information

June 30, 2017 Instructions for xxxx in the Event of Bob's Death:

1. Contact attorney's office immediately, provide him with a copy of the will and ask him to make a copy and return ASAP. Original will is in safe. He should handle (and be paid for) all aspects of the estate and will guide & instruct you what to do.
2. My tools, my Dad's watch, my Dad's xxxx, my xxxx should immediately go to xxx. Notify car/home/life/health insurance of my death. Ryan please don't sell the xxxx ever-pass it on to your son or daughter and do not allow them to sell it either because xxxxx.
3. Advisors: Legal-xxxx, Insurance: xxxx, Tax: xxxx Contact them all within a few days of death. See the life insurance electronic file in OneDrive-Personal (Financial info) for detailed life insurance information.
4. Contact Social Security Administration. You are eligible for reduced widow benefits now, but I suggest waiting until you reach age 66 and sign up for widow's benefit because you don't need it until then. You will need my date of birth xxxx, social security # off of tax return, your own passport and driver's license, wedding license copy from safe and death certificate
5. Sign up for Medicare at 65-it is not automatic. Go to www.Medicare.gov 3 months before 65 to sign up
6. Have the funeral home provide you with 15 original death certificates.
7. xxxx will receive approximately xxxx in life insurance, I suggest you use the money as follows:
    a. Payoff any credit cards-no other personal debt exists except monthly credit cards.
    b. xxxx
    c. Continue your health insurance through COBRA until you qualify for Medicare at 65. Make sure to keep paying your long-term care insurance premium every quarter to Northwestern Mutual-call xxxx with questions.
    d. Roll my retirement accounts into a new IRA for you. Do not take any of the retirement money until at least age 70 if you can hold off-for emergencies hit the cd's. You will have approximately xxxx in retirement money from both of us-ask xxxx for advice.
    e. Consider with xxxx what to do with real estate.
8. Bury me in the cheapest possible casket. Do not waste any money on a fancy casket, elaborate services, etc.
    a. Bury me in a polo shirt from Kapalua, shorts and tennis shoes-I'm going to play golf there at Kapalua in heaven. Have a farewell celebration not a wake. I have had a wonderful life-xxxxx Play xxxx at the conclusion of any services.
    b. I want a xxxx service and funeral, and want to be buried in a xxxx cemetery.

Tab 1: Banking Information

This tab should have a simple list showing the bank name, address and account number of every bank or credit union checking or savings account. It should state the branch where you normally bank and any individuals with whom you normally deal. It should state whether there is a debit card associated with the account, whether it is interest-bearing or not, and who has signature authority over the account. Examples are in *italics.* List every checking, savings, or other account with any financial institution. Also list accounts held for children or others.

Bank & Type of account	Address	Acct#	Branch & Employee	Debit Card?	Interest bearing?	Signatories
Chase-checking						Joint
Chase-savings						Joint
Chase-Money Market						Joint
First Savings CD						Joint
Xx Jr savings						Just Bob

Consider including recent account statements as backup for these accounts. Also once again provide guidance on where the registers are for these accounts, if any, and a detailed list of automatic withdrawals by: Payee; purpose; date; amount. Provide as much information as possible because your survivor may not know anything about these deals.

Example List of automatic withdrawals and deposits:

- *Paychecks for xxx and yyy are direct deposited every pay day into Chase checking xxx. Pay days are the 15th and 30th of every month for xxx and every Friday for yyy.*
- *Our car payment is withdrawn on the 5th of every month from Chase checking account xxx in the amount of $zzzz. This is a 48 month, 0% interest car loan taken out on July 1, 2015 to buy the 2014 Dodge Ram.*
- *Our home mortgage is withdrawn on the 9th of every month from Chase checking account xxx in the amount of $zzz. This is a 20-year mortgage taken out on January 11, 2008. The monthly payment of zzz includes escrow of ffff which pays for home insurance and property tax.*
- *There are no other automatic withdrawals from this or any other account.*

Tab 2. Financial Information

Ideally the financial tab will be a hyperlinked Excel balance sheet that lists everything you own in the main categories shown, with account numbers, related loan payoffs and account numbers, and the amount of monthly payment. It will also reflect the last date each amount was verified. I have reprinted an example Excel balance sheet below.

The second page of the financial tab should be a summary budget for the year, not a detailed budget, although I suggest including your detailed budgets on the third pages since this book is now our central reference point for all financial decisions.

Page 1 of Financial Tab

XXXX and YYYY											
PERSONAL FINANCIAL STATEMENT											
12/31/2016											
	ASSETS				Confirmed	RELATED LIABILITIES					Last Date
CASH:						DESCRIPTION	Acct No.	BALANCE DUE	MO. PMT	Payoff	Verified
Cash on Hand			$0			NONE					
Checking-Chase			0			NONE					
Fidelity Investment Account			0			NONE					
	TOTAL CASH			$0							
STOCKS, BONDS-PUBLIC COMPANIES											
	TOTAL STOCKS, BONDS			$0							
PENSIONS											
IRA-Fidelity		Mr	$0			NONE					
Cash Value Life		Joint	0			NONE					
	TOTAL PENSIONS			$0							
PRIVATE INVESTMENTS											
	TOTAL PRIVATE			$0							
REAL ESTATE											
	TOTAL REAL ESTATE			$0							
PERSONAL PROPERTY											
	TOTAL PERSONAL PROP.			$0		TOTAL LIABILITIES		$0			
						NET WORTH		$0			
TOTAL ASSETS				$0		TOTAL LIAB + NET WORTH		$0			

Most values in the first 3 sections should be exact and agree with related supporting statements from where you have the money. The last 3 categories are all estimates-be conservative and you can also use this as a financial statement to give to your local banker if you ever need to borrow money.

The cash section should show any type of account held with a bank or credit union. You could also include brokerage accounts here, but I like listing them separately in the next category of stocks and bonds. If you have a brokerage account just show the total value on your most recent statement, there is no need to list individual holdings.

Under the pension heading list any type of retirement account at the total value of the pensions by individual and then by the account trustee. For example, if Ryan and Casey each have pensions at Vanguard and Fidelity it might look something like this:

Type	*Holder*	*Trustee*	*Value*	*As of*	*Beneficiary*
IRA	Casey	Fidelity	21,000	12/31/16	Ryan
401k	Casey	Vanguard	7,000	12/31/16	Ryan
Roth IRA	Ryan	Vanguard	12,000	06/30/17	Casey
401k	Ryan	Fidelity	17,000	06/30/17	Casey

Private investments would be the value of any ownership you might have in a personal or closely held business. Be very conservative on values.

Real estate values should be a realistic estimate of what your home (and other property) would sell for on the date of the statement.

The personal property section is where you would include things like jewelry, collectibles, furniture, coins, cars, etc. List car loans and credit card balances here as liabilities too.

Page 2 of FInancial Tab

		Estimated 2017
ESTIMATED INCOME		
XXXX Job 1		$0
XXXX Job 2		0
YYYY Job 1		0
Other		0
	TOTAL INCOME	$0
EXPENSES		
Home Mortgage		0
Car Payment XXXX		0
Car Repairs, Insurance, Plates & Gas		0
Food & Clothing		0
Charity		0
Entertainment		0
Investments		0
Vacation		0
Insurance		0
Utilities & Telephone		0
Miscellaneous		0
Retirement		0
Home Insurance		0
Property Tax		0
Other		0
	TOTAL EXPENSES	$0
	DIFFERENCE	$0

The detail of Page 2 should use net pay and should be summary amounts only. Detailed breakdowns of income and expense would be in the detailed budgets that follow, this should just be a summary of the current or coming year for both your survivors as well as for banking and long-term budgeting purposes.

TAB 3 Retirement

This tab should provide detail of every account by individual, with a summary page showing fair values, beneficiaries, and the support following in the form of your most recent statement from the retirement trustee. Make sure that the statements show account numbers, addresses, phone numbers, and a detail of the holdings inside of the retirement account. The first page summary should agree with the numbers on the financial statement in Tab 2. Remember, the purpose of this book is to help your heirs, so plenty of information needs to be available here. I would also include in this section your most recent Social Security earnings statement, although I would not assign it a dollar value.

Tab 4 Insurance

This tab should be broken into several categories: home/apartment; car; life; and health/long-term care. Include a cover page for your home policy which shows the carrier, policy number, agent and contact information, policy term, levels of coverage and premium, and how the premium is paid (such as through escrow or personally). Then attach the most recent policy. I like the summary page because it forces you to look at the policy and see if it provides adequate coverage, for example does it pay replacement cost for the home *and* the contents? What about policy limits on the home or special coverage for earthquakes and floods if needed. What about liability levels? You might consider recording a cell phone video of your home or apartment, plus its contents to prove the condition and existence of items.

Car insurance should also be summarized by carrier, policy number, agent and contact information, policy term and premium, and how the premium is paid (such as monthly automatic withdrawal, or quarterly by check). Also attach a copy of the policy right after the summary page. Your car insurance should also include coverage for uninsured motorists. The decision to carry collision coverage once a car is paid for is a personal decision, because collision pays for damage you cause to your own vehicle, and a similar decision is required for comprehensive coverage. I usually carry collision coverage for paid off vehicles if they are worth more than $10,000 or so, but I retain a $1,000 deductible to keep the cost way down. I always carry comprehensive insurance on paid off vehicles, also maintaining a $1,000 deductible to keep the costs down. Comprehensive pays for your car being stolen, glass and things other than collision.

Life insurance requires a tremendous amount of detailed information regarding who the insured is, beneficiaries, policy number, carrier and contact information, as well as the face amount of the benefit, cash surrender value and outstanding loans. The physical policies must be turned in to receive the benefits, but a simple affidavit is available from most companies if the policy cannot be found. The affidavit can be used to obtain the benefits, but will add some time to receiving the proceeds. All life insurance payoffs will require a certified death certificate, so make sure to obtain several from the funeral home, as uncomfortable as that is. Social Security & Medicare will be notified by the funeral home or coroner of death, but retirement plans, health insurance, and long-term care insurance policy holders must be notified, as should joint carriers of home and car insurance.

I suggest maintaining a life insurance summary page on an Excel spreadsheet, with separate columns for each family member with the following headings, and totals under the benefit and cash value columns:

Insurer	Sponsor	Phone	Term/Whole	Payment	Due Dates	Agent	Policy Date	Policy #	[illegible]	YYY Benefit	Cash Value	Beneficiary	Last Update

Health and long-term care information should also be maintained in a detailed summary page, much like life insurance with carrier, contact information, policy numbers, etc. A copy of current health insurance cards should be included immediately after the summary page. For long-term care policies, also provide a summary of benefits on the summary page, maintaining the physical policy in a secure location, such as the fireproof safe.

Tab 5 Investments

This tab should include a summary page of account information and the location of any money invested outside of a bank or credit union, plus contact information. It should be followed by the most recent account statements (update it 2-4 times annually). The summary page total should agree with the numbers on your financial statement.

Tab 6 Other

If the needed information doesn't fit another category, put it here! When my Dad died, he left some property in a remote area and I included a map in the other tab! Other things might be copies of birth, marriage and divorce certificates and orders, military service records passport copies, a list of any contents in a safe, an inventory of household personal property, a list of social media accounts and log-ins, a list of frequent flyer accounts and accumulations and log-ins and any other unusual things that might not have a tangible dollar value but have an indeterminable value to the heirs.

10
LIFE INSURANCE AND ANNUTIES

Life insurance is bought by individuals who wish to provide for their survivor's needs, burial costs, and sometimes a transfer of wealth to a survivor. The normal answer to "How much life insurance do I need", is what do you want it to do? If you decide you want to provide for your heirs and burial needs go to http://www.bankrate.com/calculators/insurance/life-insurance-calculator.aspx as a starting point. I don't necessarily agree with their result, but it is a start.

I have seen two main mistakes made by financial advisors and life insurance sales people when determining the amount of needed life insurance. First, I have never had an agent or advisor acknowledge that upon your death your heirs will most likely receive a Social Security benefit, plus money to take care of any children under age 16 in the household. (Buy my Social Security book at https://www.amazon.com/2017-Social-Security-Guide-Jennings/dp/1542700930 .

Second, advisors always tell you to buy term and invest the difference. This is a prime example of excellent textbook advice that falls apart in the real world. In nearly 40 years of tax and financial planning practice I could count on one hand the folks that "invested the difference", so my advice will be different, controversial and real-life. I agree with the concept of buying term and investing the difference, but I disagree with the application.

Let's start by discussing the three reasons to buy life insurance. We will begin by assuming that you want at least enough insurance to provide for your internment. A few years ago the National Funeral Director's Association pegged final funeral costs at about $9,600, so let's say burial in a metal casket, with a plot and services will cost about $10,000. Changing from a metal casket to a simple wooden casket can knock $3-4,000 off of the cost (and since you are dead you won't notice the difference!). Changing to cremation will take the total cost down to about $5,000. Maybe I am being too cold, but the only person that benefits from a fancy funeral with a 100-year guaranteed life casket, elaborate headstone and magnificent service would be the funeral home. In any event let's assume that your cost of passing on will be about $10,000 for planning purposes.

Next, let's address the money your spouse will need to live on after you pass, plus the cost of caring for the kids. Costs will decrease a bit for food, clothing and insurance, but sadly the big expenses for housing, utilities and school won't change. The calculation for the amount of insurance needed is simple: add up the costs at death (about $10,000); plus, needed income replacement until retirement; plus, any additional funds you wish to leave your family, and that is how much insurance you need. Theoretically, insurance needs diminish as you age because income needs are reduced and children grow up and move away. However, don't scrimp on insurance coverage because there is no room to make a mistake here. I also want to go ahead and state that I am biased in favor of buying insurance, including whole or universal life insurance, as discussed later.

Let's go back to Matt and Valerie in Chapter 2. It looks like they are living on about $50,000 annually of after tax income, and they are newly married in their late 20's. They have one child, Piper, and may have one more. If Matt dies in a horrible filing cabinet tragedy at the tax office Valerie will need $50,000 every year according to conventional thinking. If you go to the bankrate website previously quoted, plug-in $10,000 for burial costs, 35 years for the period of time the money will be needed until social security kicks in and 2 kids going to college, it tells Matt he needs about $1 million in life insurance. What this and most other websites ignore is the Social Security benefit his survivors will receive.

Based on Matt's work history, if he is savagely and fatally injured by a slamming file drawer, each of his 2 kids will receive about $1200 a month from Social Security until they are age 18, and his widow Valerie will receive about $1600 per month until the youngest child turns 16. This is $4,000 monthly for at least 16 years, or about what Valerie and the kids will need to live on, not counting burial costs. There won't be any extra money, but if they must, they should only get enough insurance to wrap him in some newspapers, stick him in a hole, and say a prayer in the Wal-Mart parking lot. Heck, Valerie will also receive a $250 death benefit from Social Security when he goes.

Matt however, wants his family to have more than the minimum, be able to pay for college for the current and coming child, and be able to not struggle if he passes on. A happy medium here would be for Matt to try to buy about ½ of the estimated needed insurance, or about $500,000. Matt gets $50,000 term coverage paid for through work, so he needs another $400-500,000 in insurance. The question is, should he buy term and "invest the difference" or do something else? The only flaw in the "buy term and invest the difference" format is that he is buying insurance only, but receiving no investment or tax benefit in return. www.tiaa.org shows that Matt's monthly cost for a $500,000 term policy is $17.50, or for a $1 million dollar term policy is $28.00. Not bad at all.

Whole or universal life policies are policies that build a cash value over time using the premiums paid, and after 5-7 years the growth in cash value is generally far in excess of the premium paid. As a simple rule of thumb however, these policies cost about ten times more per year than term life, and the expenses of the whole life policy for "surrender charges" and the like are substantial. ***Financially, buying term is Matt's best idea if he***

can take the rest (or 150 to 250 per month from our example) and invest it in a stable growth investment. Sadly, my experience shows me that is quite unlikely that Matt will invest the difference. Insurance agents use the "forced savings" concept as a sales tool for whole life insurance, and get ripped apart in the financial press, but as a non-licensed professional that understands how most Americans really operate, I still like whole life for three reasons: first, it is a forced investment, granted; second it builds cash value in a tax-free manner that you can access at any time after the first 5 or so years; and third upon payout it is also tax-free. My real-life advice to Matt would be to buy the $500,000 cheap term policy and consider buying a $500,000 whole or universal policy while he is young.

On a side note, whole life policies are at their cheapest when you are at your youngest. As a grandparent/parent buying whole life policies on my kids and grandkids has been a way for me to transfer wealth to my kids and grandkids in a tax-free manner while providing them protection, For example, I bought a $250,000 whole life policy on my grandson when he turned one from Northwestern Mutual (I get no commissions from them!) for about $1,200 annually. Once he hits age six the cash value will be growing faster than the premium every year, the premium will not increase, he has a guaranteed ability to buy more, in an emergency he can access the cash value, and I do not have a taxable transfer to him.

In summary, I absolutely agree that buying term life insurance and investing the difference is the best financial aspect of buying life insurance, but the real decisions made in life make the forced investment characteristics of whole-life insurance a valid consideration in the purchase of insurance, so I like a mix of the two types of insurance.

<u>Annuities</u>

Annuities are investments made in insurance-like policies that provide a steady stream of income to the purchaser or their heirs. With an immediate annuity the payments start immediately and can be paid monthly, quarterly or annually. With a deferred annuity the payments start at some policy-defined date in the future.

Unlike most accountants I am not in the "annuities are horrible" boat, but rather I am in the "annuities are often bad" boat. In general, annuities offer guaranteed rates of return at lower risk than direct investments, professional management, and tax deferral, but are subject to horrendous fees for early surrender, high annual management, the risk of bankruptcy of the annuity company and the inability to get all your money back for seven years. The costs of an annuity end up being about three times higher than the purchase of equivalent mutual fund investments because of the fees. Frankly, no-load mutual funds from Vanguard offer just as good as an investment without the additional fees, meaning you automatically are ahead of the earnings game up-front and every year.

When you buy an annuity, you are paying a commission to someone whose company will then also indirectly charge you a management fee that is 200-300% higher than the normal industry asset management fees, and who won't give you all your money back for seven years if you change your mind. If you want someone else to invest for you through an annuity, please recognize that you are paying 3 to 4% annually for that privilege. Are you sure you want this?

If you still wish to buy an annuity, the only ones I would recommend would be those bought as "direct-sold", or commission-free annuities from Vanguard, TIAA or the like. Never buy an annuity inside an IRA because the main advantage of the annuity of tax-free growth already occurs inside the IRA, so you are paying exorbitant fees for a benefit you already receive! If you are still working for an employer that offers a 401K plan you should never buy an annuity until you have deferred the maximum allowed into the 401K plan because the 401K plan offers the exact same advantage of tax deferral without the horrendous fees or loss of liquidity.

Exchanging an existing annuity for a new one is usually tax-free, but re-subjects you to a new set of surrender charges, fees, etc., and provides the sales agent with a generous 5-8% commission (that the annuity company must earn back before you get anything), meaning the only winner on an annuity exchange is the salesman!

In summary, I believe annuities should be purchased only by people wishing to pay the highest investment management fees in America to give their money to someone who will penalize them for 7 years if they want their money back, while continuing to charge the buyer an annual management fee before the buyer earns anything. My sarcasm runneth over on annuities.

A Final Note

Thank you for buying "Paid For". Mr. Johnson in my office prodded me to write this book, and even though it is clearly biased, I hope it is informational but more importantly, useful. Thank you Mr. Johnson. Over the last 40 years I learned to tell people what they needed to hear, not what they wanted to hear and I hope it has been duplicated for you in this book. As I say in our seminars, you won't agree with everything I say, get past that, and keep listening because there is still some great stuff in here!

Email ideas or suggestions to my office at BobJ@Taxspeaker.com and look for the small business version of "Paid For" in the near future.

Paid For Action Checklist:

Action	Date Completed
One Time Actions	
Buy 3-ring Binder and Develop "The Life Book"	
Prepare after-death instructions	
Will Preparation	
Medical Directive for Wills	
Durable Power of Attorney	
Install Quicken or Mint software to track everything	
Have 1st family meeting and establish short and long term goals	
Prepare first detailed budget	
Prepare initial financial statement on Excel	
Prepare initial life insurance summary on Excel	
Prepare health insurance summary	
Prepare initial home or apartment insurance summary	
Inventory home or apartment contents & video record	
Prepare retirement plan summary	
Prepare first detailed budget	
Cut up all but 1 credit card and put it in a safe place *AT HOME*	
Get a second job if needed for debt reduction or goals	
Enroll in employer 401K, deferring at least 6%	
Enroll in applicable employer cafeteria plans	

Paid for

Determine life insurance needs for both spouses	
Purchase 50% term, 50% whole life as previously determined	
Obtain and review your Social Security earnings statements	
Move (or establish) Coverdell ESA savings for children	
Every Quarter	
Family meeting to go over budget & goals & adjust them	
Prepare new budget	
Every Six Months	
Update financial statements	
Update retirement account spreadsheets	
Annually (as a minimum)	
Update life insurance spreadsheets	
Update health insurance spreadsheets	
Increase 401K deferral	
Evaluate and adjust cafeteria plan deferrals	

ABOUT THE AUTHOR

Bob Jennings was originally licensed as a Certified Public Accountant in Colorado in 1980 after graduating with a Masters Degree in Accounting from Colorado State University. He is an actively licensed CPA in Indiana, an IRS Enrolled Agent (EA) and was a (now retired) Certified Financial Planner for over 20 years. He lives in Indiana and Florida with his wife of over 40 years, and is also the founder and President of TaxSpeaker®, a national financial continuing education company. In his spare time Bob restores old Mopar muscle cars and was the subject of articles in Hemmings & Fiat/Chrysler publications about his one-man drive in his Nascar-inspired 1970 Plymouth Superbird race car from Louisville, Kentucky to Whittier, Alaska in 2015.

66358799R00055

Made in the USA
Lexington, KY
11 August 2017